# MY TWENTIETH CENTURY

# MY TWENTIETH CENTURY

## BY

### Hazel Andrews Reed

*Hazel Andrews Reed*
*Nov. 1997*

Published by Rainbow's End Company
354 Golden Grove Road
Baden, PA 15005

EMail Address: BTucker833@aol.com
http://adpages.com/rbebooks

Cover Design: Sue Vincent

Note: Hazel Andrews Reed, the author, is the first person on the
left side of the cover.

ISBN: 1-880451-29-8

Library of Congress Catalog Card Number: 97-76660

Dedicated

to my family and friends

and

to those sharing and living the twentieth century with me who
have made a positive difference that will
influence future generations.

## Special Acknowledgment

I would like to thank Thomas A. Liston, my nephew, who was instrumental in getting my life story together. His hard work and encouragement in bringing about the fulfillment of this project is deeply appreciated.

# Table of Contents

# Preface

This century, to me, has been the most productive in the history of man. Being a teacher, I found that the profession was a reward in itself, but I also had a sincere desire to know a greater number of people and to get better acquainted with other geographical areas of this world. Travel appeared to be the answer. But, no matter where my lifetime travels took me, I always maintained a special bond with Enon Valley in Pennsylvania where my roots are forever planted.

While getting my teeth cleaned in the dentist's office, I questioned the hygienist, "How many patients do you have who are 93 and still have their own teeth?"

She responded, "We don't have any other 93-year-old patients—period!"

The following lines, although not my creation, seem to effectively express my present position:

> When I was young, my slippers were red
> And I could kick as high as my head.
> As I got older, my slippers were blue
> And I could dance the whole night through.
> Now that I'm old, my slippers are black
> And it's hard to walk to the corner and back!
>
> Author Unknown

This book was written to review, select and consolidate the highlights of my "twentieth century" and is offered to readers as my last major labor of love.

*Today, as I look toward my next birthday, memories of a long and eventful life rush through my mind. Here, these memories, along with tales told by my forbearers, give readers a presentation of my twentieth century . . .*

# PART I

## Enon Valley, Pennsylvania

Enon Valley, Pennsylvania is a very special town to me. Leaving the Andrews farm, which had been in the family for several generations, my family moved to Enon Valley in 1904 when I was one year of age. The house we moved into that day was to be our family home for more than fifty years. The Andrews family originated in Ireland, when Samuel Andrews married Elizabeth Chambers. The couple immigrated to America, settling in western Pennsylvania. Among their children was John Andrews, my great-grandfather, who married Elizabeth Harnett.

The first settlers came in the spring of 1796. A great deal of the land was secured through donation and/or depreciation. Land speculators, for as little as three cents an acre, bought much of the land in this area from soldiers being discharged from the Revolutionary War. These men then banded together and came to this wild area to claim the land. Working long hours, they felled trees, built cabins, and cleared enough land for their farm buildings and gardens. Wild animals, grey wolves, turkey, deer, beaver, big toe panthers, rattlesnakes and bears were prevalent and it was important that the land around their cabins be cleared. Children could not play outdoors without supervision.

Many of the residents who live in this area today are the direct descendants of those same brave men. Among the original settlers were:

| | |
|---|---|
| Samuel Andrews | John Severs Madden |
| James McCowin | James Stevenson McKean |
| William Robinson | Robert Johnston McCarter |
| Andrew Moore | John Wilson Rainey |
| Philip Aughenbaugh | John Taylor Harnett |
| Thomas Smith | John Marshall Wallace |
| Joseph Smith | David Clark |
| William Porter | Thomas Dalzel long |
| John Beers | Enoch Marvin Wurtsel |

This group of men were called "The Settlers of 96." Under the Settlement Act of the late 1700's the Pennsylvania Population Company obtained 100,000 acres of land in the Enon area. This area was a wilderness, populated by an abundance of Indians, and timbered with oak, hickory, maple, poplar, chestnut, and other deciduous vegetation.

To take advantage of the water power, the early settlers built mills in the lowland area surrounding Little Beaver Creek.

During the winter months of 1796, these men returned to the east of Pittsburgh and Uniontown to stay with their families. In the early spring of 1797 they returned, bringing their families with them to settle in the new cabins.

John Beers, one of the few men who could read and write, served as what, today, we would call a Justice of the Peace. He had no stamp to verify his position; however, on every document, following his signature, was a special verification mark. That special mark can clearly be seen on a deed for transfer of land by Samuel Harnett that is shown on page 15.

John Beers' wife died during that first winter, the winter of 1797, and he donated three acres of his farm to establish a cemetery there. That was the beginning of Little Beaver Cemetery.

John and Elizabeth Harnett Andrews—my great-grandparents were among the first to settle in the virgin forests of western Pennsylvania in an area several miles from a navigable stream.

Andrews Family Farm Home

They settled there at the time when soldiers who had served in the Revolutionary War, in compensation for their service, were being given land grants in this wild country. The number of acres they received depended upon their rank and length of service. Many of these soldiers, rather than face the rigors of developing land they knew little or nothing about, were glad to part with their acreage for a few cents an acre.

The land was divided according to rank, and there were four sizes of lots. First class lots were for 500 acres; second class, 300 acres; third class, 250 acres; fourth class, 200 acres. In addition, there was an allowance of six percent to provide for roads. The amount of land allotted to each person was as follows:

| **Rank** | **Lot** | **Acres** |
|---|---|---|
| Major General | 4 first class | 2,000 |
| Brigadier General | 3 first class | 1,500 |
| Colonel | 2 first class | 1,000 |
| Lt. Colonel | 1 first class<br>1 second class | 800 |
| Surgeon, Chaplain or Major | 2 second class | 600 |
| Captain | 1 first class | 500 |
| Lieutenant | 2 fourth class | 400 |
| Ensign or Regimental Surgeon's Mate | 1 second class | 300 |
| Sergeant or Sergeant Major or Quartermaster Sergeant | 1 third class | 250 |
| Drum Major or Fife Major Drummer or Fifer Corporal or Private | 1 fourth class | 200 |

None of this acreage was distributed in Little Beaver Township. Although some farmers in North Beaver Township have papers verifying their claim to their farms, I have been unable to determine how my forbearers acquired their land.

Deed for the Andrews' Farm

A story about a doctor and his bride illustrates some of the hardships suffered by these brave early settlers. The couple came from Connecticut to settle in Darlington, about four miles from Enon Valley. The long trip from Connecticut took them through heavily forested country and across rugged mountains. Along the way, the young bride became completely disillusioned and longed for the green hills of Connecticut. Continuing to brood, she wasted away and eventually died. Her young husband realized the kindest thing he could do for her was to return her body to the beautiful countryside she loved so much. So, sealing her remains in a barrel of whiskey, he loaded it aboard a stage coach, and had his bride returned to Connecticut for burial!

While researching for a church anniversary some years ago, we uncovered the following interesting information. The Little Beaver Presbyterian Church was organized around 1838. It was a mile or so from the town of Enon Valley and quite near the Little Beaver Cemetery. One of the pillars of the church was a man of some means. He paid for one of the most desirable pews—as was the custom—and supported the church financially in numerous ways. However, he was believed to be fond of alcohol—so much so that a friend reported on his activities near a bar in Beaver Falls. As he came out of the bar, it was noted that he had a red nose, his speech was slurred; and, as he walked down the street, he couldn't seem to follow a straight course. This was reported to the church fathers. Following consultation with a higher church body, the Presbytery, he was relieved of his office in the local church.

After the Fort Wayne and Chicago Railroad came through Enon Valley around 1850, another Presbyterian church was constructed in the village. Among the officers helping to launch the new church was none other than the gentleman who had been ostracized from the Little Beaver Church. *Could it be because he was a man of means?*

The arrival of the railroad preceded many changes. Before

young men arrived in Enon as telegraph operators. One telegraph office was in the railroad station. The other was in a tower
near the rail line, between , Enon Valley (our town) and New
Galilee. All such towers probably had letter names—this was
known as K Y.

The two young men, referred to above, later married my
father's two sisters, Lily and Mamie. That ended their days on the
farm!

As work on the railroad progressed; and the company bought
their right-of-way, a certain segment of the population in the area
tried to prevent the railroad from happening. These were local
men with a team of horses and a wagon who made their living
hauling coal and other items for the local population. Of course,
their's was a losing battle. When I was a little girl, there were still
men in Enon with teams of horses and wagons who were doing
local hauling.

People resorted to many means to make a living. A farmer
who raised geese or ducks for market had no means to get them
to the Beaver Valley towns or Pittsburgh markets. Following the
arrival of the railroad, the farmers would clip the feathers of one
wing of the duck or goose ready for market and drive them on
foot to Enon or New Galilee where they were loaded on specially
equipped cars to be transported to market. Trucks had not yet
been invented and there were no hard roads.

When Elizabeth Andrews suffered a broken hip, there were
no doctors in the area. According to my Aunt Mamie, at night the
family would make her as comfortable as possible in bed and,
during the day, place her on a comfortable chair near the fire where
she would sew, quilt, knit, and prepare vegetables for their meals.
Mamie was seventeen when her Grandmother Elizabeth died at
age eighty-four.

John and Elizabeth Andrews became the parents of ten
children. My grandfather, Martin Luther Andrews, was the seventh child born to the family. He married Kate Talbert Young, a
tailor and dressmaker from Youngstown, Ohio. Since Martin taught

school, Kate probably pictured them living in a nice comfortable home somewhere near Youngstown. Instead, he brought her to his home—the Andrews farm—where his still unmarried brothers and sisters were also living. Kate had a beautiful wardrobe when she married; however, she quickly became pregnant and was unable to wear any of her lovely clothes and her sisters-in-law inherited them.

At that time it was traditional that the older sisters in a family be married before the younger ones. Two of the younger sisters, Harriet and Margaret Andrews, had beaux courting them and wanted to get married. Resourcefully they located a husband, Snyder A. McNutt, for their older sister Isabelle.

Snyder and Isabelle, who prospered as farmers, had two children, Lois and John. When they were older, they decided to replace the house in which they had lived for so many years. Unfortunately, Snyder died before the new house was finished. At that time it was the custom for funerals to be held in the home of the person who had died. They postponed his funeral for a week while they finished the new house. I sometimes wonder if, during this time, Isabelle used the whiskey-barrel method of preservation!

In a double wedding ceremony Margaret Andrews married Leander McCauley; and, her sister, Harriet M. Andrews, married Cyrus Guy.

Cyrus attended Washington and Jefferson College in Washington, Pennsylvania. After graduating, he was hired by a wealthy Virginia plantation owner as a tutor for his children. Unfortunately for Cyrus, this was during the Civil War; and he was conscripted to serve in the Confederate Army. When the war ended, he then returned home and married Harriet. Cyrus Guy is the only Confederate soldier to be buried in the Little Beaver Cemetery.

William James Wells Andrews, the oldest of the M.L. Andrews siblings, returned from the Spanish American War and, notwithstanding the fact that this was 50 years after gold was discovered in California, was certain that his future lay in searching for gold. Somehow he persuaded his dad, my grandfather, to give him the money from the sale of their wheat crop for the trip. How my grandfather and his family survived without the money from this cash crop we'll never know.

My uncle made it to California and, at the time of the 1906 earthquake, was living in the San Francisco area . The following post card photos are a sign that the folks back home tried to keep in touch with him.

Post Card from Will Andrews

VIEW OF RUINS OF RETAIL DISTRICT OF SAN FRANCISCO AFTER THE GREAT EARTHQUAKE AND FIRE, APRIL 18-21, 1906

Post Card from Will Andrews

Will, not finding gold in California, moved to Chicago and became a butcher. There he acquired a wife, Effie, and had at least four children—twins Cecelia and Findley, Floria and Iola. At that time Chicago seemed as far from western Pennsylvania as California seems today; but, in an attempt to stay informed about Will and his family, my mother corresponded regularly with Aunt Effie. In one of her letters Aunt Effie informed the family that Will had left—disappeared.

We learned later that he had moved back to California where

he married and fathered another family—a daughter Gail, a son, Will Jr., and at least two other children. Again, when the going got rough, Will got going, and he soon disappeared from this, his second family.

After World War II, when Will Jr. was a patient in a Veterans Hospital in California, he frequently received mail for another Will Andrews—mail that obviously wasn't for him. He finally looked up the other Will Andrews—a patient in the same hospital—the other Will Andrews was his father! What a tragedy—or travesty!

Gail said that, for her, it would have been better if her dad had not been found. She also said that during her growing up years, her mother believed in her heart that her husband and the father of her children had not deserted them. She was certain he had met with foul play.

But Will was back! In fact, he spent most of the summer of 1946 with his Andrews kin in western Pennsylvania. In 1947 or 1948, after Uncle Howard Buttermore's death, Aunt Mamie Andrews Buttermore, Will's youngest sister, moved to California where she got in touch with Will and revived their brother-sister relationship. She also got acquainted with some of his children. His oldest daughter, Gail, was married and had a good job with the YWCA. Her husband, a doctor, enlisted in Canada and was severely wounded during the war. He convalesced in a Veterans Hospital in Canada. In the late fifties, Gail moved east and was on assignment with the YWCA in Gloversville, New York. One weekend she came down to Hempstead, New York to spend a weekend with Jack Quinn, my first husband, and myself. We intended to pursue the relationship with her but it never happened. Will Sr. lived to be in his late nineties—as did Aunt Emma and Aunt Mamie.

John Calvin Guy Andrews, the second son of M. L. and Kate Andrews, was the quiet one. In 1895, he married Kate Boyd and they had one daughter, Marguerite. She married Stanley

Veon and they were the parents of six children: Paul, Kathryn, Roy, Ralph, Lloyd and Ruth. The Boyd farm adjoined the Andrews farm. John, in addition to tilling the Boyd acreage, also had a saw mill where he did custom work. He prospered and eventually was able to build a modern home in Enon where they spent their winters. During the summer months, they lived on the Boyd farm. At times, my father, George Andrews, worked with or for Uncle John at the saw mill.

Emma Florence Andrews married Erastus Matthew Faddis, and they lived in Canton, Ohio for many years. Later, Uncle Ras became a crackerjack salesman with the Hoover Sweeper Company and was transferred to different localities in the South; however, Guy, their son, stayed in the Canton area for most of his working years. Once a year or so, he would visit us in Enon usually arriving on the late afternoon train and leaving the next day on the early morning train. We loved to have him visit. He had such a good sense of humor and played the piano so beautifully. Guy married Velma Robinson, and they had two daughters, Lucy and Eleanor. Later Guy and Velma divorced, and Guy ended up in California with Clif—a man of questionable reputation.

Later, after Uncle Ras' death, Guy assumed responsibility for his mother. After retiring from the Timken Roller Bearing Company in Canton, Guy and his mother moved to New Smyrna Beach, Florida. When Aunt Emma's mind failed, Guy was forced to put her in a nursing home where she lived for some time. Eventually, when Guy's own health failed, his younger daughter, Eleanor, took over. He died of cancer in the late sixties. Guy and Clif were close to Aunt Mamie and Uncle Howard. More on that story later . . .

Anna Andrews married John Fredrick Winter of Petersburg, Ohio. We called him Uncle Jess. He loved poetry and was at his best when he could recite the many poems he had memorized. Uncle Jess took up housekeeping on the north side of Pittsburgh where he was a blacksmith—a trade much in demand in an era that preceded cars and trucks. At times, his customers would pay him with goods. I can vividly recall some beautiful solid mahogany furniture that he received in this way. Later, he opened a shop in Coraopolis, Pennsylvania, where he tempered steel and repaired and replaced springs. Another move took them to Youngstown, Ohio. Uncle Jess and Aunt Anna had two children, Hazel Marie and John Fredrick. John, at the age of twelve, died suddenly of spinal meningitis. Hazel Marie developed St. Vitus Dance in her early teens and was brought to Enon where she lived in our home for several months to convalesce. She also had a chronic heart condition. She married Allen Craig, and with their son, also named John, moved to Orlando, Florida. They thought that the move to Florida might improve her health; however, her health continued to deteriorate and, in 1962, she was buried on her sixty-fifth birthday.

George Roy Andrews—my father, married Clara Rebecca McCown in 1900 and had four children: myself—Hazel Viola, Florence Ruth, Arthur Addison, and Ada Rebecca. Ada died at birth. In 1904 Dad established his business in Enon dealing in farm machinery, fencing, fertilizer, buggies, and other things. In addition, he earned money by blasting rocks and tree stumps from farmers' fields. Dad, with the help of a balky white horse named Freddy, hauled his dynamite, dynamite caps, and the other equipment he needed for this work in what we called a "cracky" wagon. It was not until late in Dad's life that I learned that the tree stumps came from virgin timber.

The picture on the following page depicts the first place of business of George R. Andrews. Clearly seen in the picture are a large group of farmers—genuine dirt-farmers—plowing, one furrow at a time, behind a team of horses. The buggies in the background date the scene as being around 1912—the Model T Days. These farmers, who didn't know the meaning of an eight hour day, made a living keeping horses, a few cows, some pigs, chickens and a big garden; thus, they provided for much of their own food.

Dad's Spring Opening 1910-1911
Identity of Persons in Picture: Arthur (brother), Ruth (author's sister),
Hazel (the author), John Andrews (Uncle), Grandfather Andrews,
George Andrews (father) Grandfather McCown

Dad's Garage, the Old Mill

Now, four or five generations later, farming has become totally mechanized with tractors, gang plows and harrows, and other equipment replacing the old till methods. Today, a farmer attending a farm implement show, would probably be wearing a Stetson hat, leather jacket, custom-made shirt, and cowboy boots. I recall our first telephone, electricity in the house, a bathroom, running water in the kitchen and a furnace. Since then technology has brought radio, TV, computers, cell telephones, and fax machines, just to name but a few. A farmer today usually has an outside job, income from government subsidies, plus an enclosed cab on the tractor to furnish heat or air-conditioning as needed. In the farmhouse, electrical conveniences have revolutionized the farm wife's role. One example is the refrigerator/freezer which has replaced the canning method of preserving food.

The large frame building that housed Dad's business had been a grist mill. We used to refer to it as *the mill;* however, after automobiles came along, it was a garage.

Family Home, Enon Valley, Pa

Dad's first car was a one-cylinder Cadillac, a roadster. He hired a blacksmith to bolt a buggy seat to the triangular shaped back area, and that is where we three kids rode. One day, he drove across a railroad crossing rather fast and I bounced out of the seat! I remember how quickly he stopped and ran back to see if I was hurt. However, I was more concerned about my dolly being damaged than about myself.

Our next car, a four-cylinder Reo, had no starter and had to be cranked by hand. It also had no windshield. I recall making a visit to Niagara Falls in it. When we ran into a sudden afternoon shower, Dad just pulled off the road and into a farmer's barn until the rain stopped.

I purchased my first car while I was teaching in Enon. It, of course, was a Ford. Dad took out the support under the front seat so that I, along with my friend Martha Anderson, could sleep in it on our planned summer vacation trip to Chicago. We planned on stopping and sleeping in the car twenty miles or so outside of Chicago; however, when we got that close, we were already in built up suburbs. As I recall, we only slept one night in the car.

We stopped at schools to use the privy and the pump, and carried a kerosene stove to cook on. Ours was the original recreation vehicle! In Chicago we went into a bank on Michigan Avenue to cash some travelers checks. We must have looked like real country bumpkins. Outside the bank, the street was decked out in bright bunting, and a parade was about to begin. I asked the banker what was going on, and he told us that Amelia Earhart was in town and the parade was in her honor. Then, looking at us with a big grin, said, "Did you girls think it was for you?"

It was our intention to try and find Uncle Will's family but, we were so taken by the city, did nothing to find them. We did, however, locate the relatives of Martha Anderson living on a one quarter section of farmland that they had claimed years before. They were doing well on the farm. We stayed one night with them

G. R. Andrews and Family in REO

Martha Anderson With R. V.

and then headed to Man, West Virginia, where my sister had just given birth to her second child, Thomas Andrews Liston. We then returned to Enon.

In the summer of 1933, I, along with three fellow teachers from New Castle, made a 10,400 mile tour to California and return. To finance the trip, each of my traveling companions paid me 1 1/4 cents a mile. One incident worth remembering happened on a Friday evening at the North Rim of the Grand Canyon in Arizona. We had stopped for our evening meal at the lodge and were amazed that we had to pay eighty-five cents for our dinner. Taking exception to this exorbitant price, I told the cashier that we hadn't paid that much since leaving Pittsburgh. However, when she told us that all the food for the lodge had to be trucked in, a distance of more than 100 miles, I stopped protesting. Transportation and refrigeration have come a long way since 1933. *I wonder what a dinner costs in that area today?*

The people at the lodge urged us to stay over until Sunday. At that time there was a group of CCC boys working in the valley at the bottom of the Canyon. They were to be brought up Saturday evening to attend a dance and, because there were so few girls, we agreed to stay. We never had so many tag dances! Whenever one of the boys drank too much beer and got drunk, the M.P.'s would put him on one of the trucks. Then, when they had a full load, would take them back to camp.

Some years after this trip, one of my co-travelers was accused of unacceptable behavior in the classroom and had to appear before the school board where the Superintendent of Schools asked her, "Did you actually hit the student?"

"Yes I did." was her honest response.

"How hard did you hit him?"

Picking up a Geography book, she hit him over the head. This action ended her teaching career.

My mother's parents' home was at Mt. Air. She had three younger brothers still at home. I fondly remember going there to visit. We were delighted when, behind a horse pulling a stone boat, we were taken to a field where, in our bare feet, we loaded stones in the boat for removal from the field. It seemed like fun—we never realized we were actually working!

My mother's parents were the McCowns. They, too, were very industrious. Grandpa worked as a blacksmith. He also, cultivated forty acres and owned several milk cows. They had a separator for the milk and took the cream to the creamery where it was made into butter. They also had a coal mine and a fruitful apple orchard on their property. Grandmother baked her bread in an outdoor oven. She also cared for their many white leghorn chickens. They had some income from the blacksmith shop, the sale of the cream, coal, eggs and apples. I recall grandmother buying a set of lovely Haviland china from the money she earned by selling apple butter made in an outdoor copper-lined kettle. Believe me, that china was used only on very special occasions!

Uncle Guy McCown, the youngest of my mother's five brothers, told me a story concerning his grandparents, who, as a young couple, had cleared the land on their farm in Little Beaver Township, Pennsylvania, to prepare it for crops. In the fall, when the crops were harvested, she would, riding horseback and leading a pack horse, take their corn and wheat to the grist mill to be ground into corn meal and flour—items essential to carry them through the winter. The forty-mile trip took two days going, one day waiting for the grain to be ground, and two days to return. No doubt, she followed streams and some poorly marked trails. The woods abounded with wild animals, and some Indians still lived in the area. I have no idea where she slept.

I can only imagine the joy and relief they must have felt when she arrived home safely following her five-day trip. Most of these settlers were devout Christians; and I can picture this young couple on their knees thanking God for her safe delivery, each other, their land, their livestock, a good crop, a warm house and the assurance that they would have provisions for the winter. Their farm was located in the soft coal area of Pennsylvania and they had a coal mine near the surface for their own use.

Martin Ray Andrews, my father's twin, lived just eight months.
Lillie May Andrews married William Langly Finefrock. They had three children, Martin Fredrick, Aletha Marie, and William Ernest—all deceased.

Mother and Father—50th Wedding Anniversary

Melvin Leander Andrews married Flossie Seltzer in 1903. Originally they lived in and around Enon, but eventually moved to Mahoningtown, and then, to be nearer to country living, moved to Mt. Jackson. Uncle Melvin worked at the cement company in Bessemer where, in 1921, after a brief illness, he died of pneumonia. Dale, their oldest son, who was a senior in high school at the time, had already been accepted at Carnegie Tech; however, feeling a responsibility to help support his mother and two younger brothers, Martin and Ralph, he found a daytime job and attended night school. Aunt Flossie had her hands full. Whenever I stopped in to see her, she was always gracious and insisted on sharing a cup of coffee or tea. One time when I was there Martin and a boarder, Mate McKim, were sitting at the dining room table discussing their future plans. When Martin said he would like to be a general in the Army, his mother said, "To be a general, you must be a leader—and you are a follower."

Martin responded, "I always lead the gang on Halloween!" He was quite artistic and, for a time, went to Clarion Normal to pursue his interest in that area.

Aunt Mamie was named Mary Bertha Andrews at birth. She married Howard Calvin Buttermore; and I must say a few words about Uncle Howard, who was an only child. Uncle Howard adopted the entire Andrews family as his own. He was a meticulous perfectionist and one of his many accomplishments was to compile the Andrews family genealogy.

Mamie and Howard were married September 16, 1903 at a time when several women in the Andrews family were pregnant and unable to attend the wedding. Lillie May gave birth to Fred Finefrock on September 23, Anna Andrews gave birth to John Winter on October 13, and Clara Andrews delivered Hazel on October 28. The family celebrated Christmas of 1903 at the Andrews farm. After dinner, the three new mothers retreated to the bedroom where, after exchanging the bonnets and blankets of their babies, called their husbands into the bedroom to see if they could identify their own baby. Needless to say, they all had a

# Ancestors of Hazel Viola Andrews

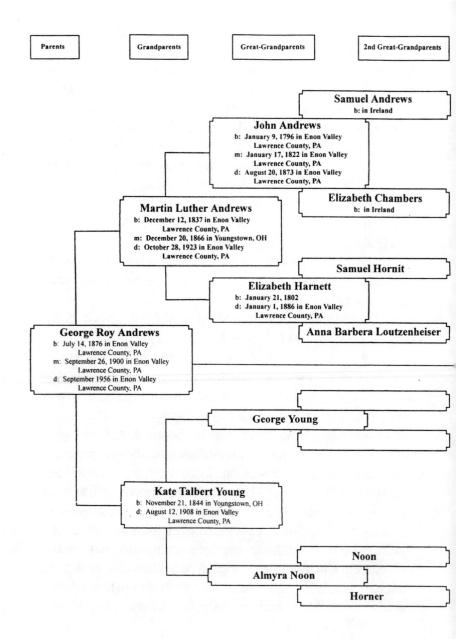

| Parents | Grandparents | Great-Grandparents | 2nd Great-Grandparents |

**Samuel Andrews**
b: in Ireland

**John Andrews**
b: January 9, 1796 in Enon Valley
Lawrence County, PA
m: January 17, 1822 in Enon Valley
Lawrence County, PA
d: August 20, 1873 in Enon Valley
Lawrence County, PA

**Elizabeth Chambers**
b: in Ireland

**Martin Luther Andrews**
b: December 12, 1837 in Enon Valley
Lawrence County, PA
m: December 20, 1866 in Youngstown, OH
d: October 28, 1923 in Enon Valley
Lawrence County, PA

**Samuel Hornit**

**Elizabeth Harnett**
b: January 21, 1802
d: January 1, 1886 in Enon Valley
Lawrence County, PA

**Anna Barbera Loutzenheiser**

**George Roy Andrews**
b: July 14, 1876 in Enon Valley
Lawrence County, PA
m: September 26, 1900 in Enon Valley
Lawrence County, PA
d: September 1956 in Enon Valley
Lawrence County, PA

**George Young**

**Kate Talbert Young**
b: November 21, 1844 in Youngstown, OH
d: August 12, 1908 in Enon Valley
Lawrence County, PA

**Noon**

**Almyra Noon**

**Horner**

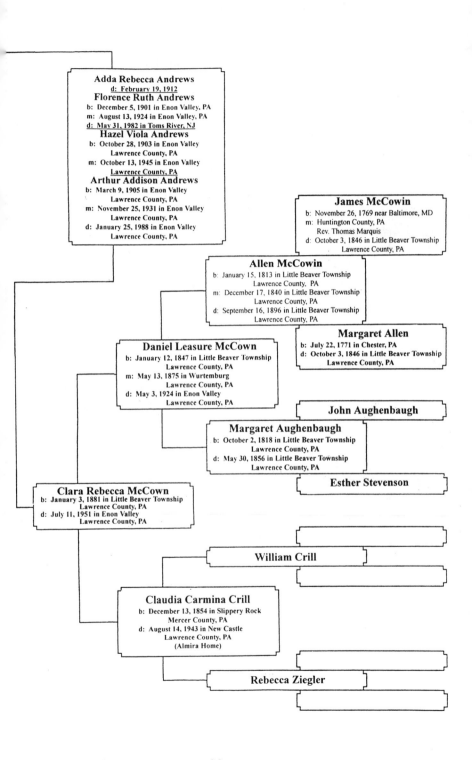

**Adda Rebecca Andrews**
d: February 19, 1912
**Florence Ruth Andrews**
b: December 5, 1901 in Enon Valley, PA
m: August 13, 1924 in Enon Valley, PA
d: May 31, 1982 in Toms River, NJ
**Hazel Viola Andrews**
b: October 28, 1903 in Enon Valley
Lawrence County, PA
m: October 13, 1945 in Enon Valley
Lawrence County, PA
**Arthur Addison Andrews**
b: March 9, 1905 in Enon Valley
Lawrence County, PA
m: November 25, 1931 in Enon Valley
Lawrence County, PA
d: January 25, 1988 in Enon Valley
Lawrence County, PA

**James McCowin**
b: November 26, 1769 near Baltimore, MD
m: Huntington County, PA
Rev. Thomas Marquis
d: October 3, 1846 in Little Beaver Township
Lawrence County, PA

**Allen McCowin**
b: January 15, 1813 in Little Beaver Township
Lawrence County, PA
m: December 17, 1840 in Little Beaver Township
Lawrence County, PA
d: September 16, 1896 in Little Beaver Township
Lawrence County, PA

**Margaret Allen**
b: July 22, 1771 in Chester, PA
d: October 3, 1846 in Little Beaver Township
Lawrence County, PA

**Daniel Leasure McCown**
b: January 12, 1847 in Little Beaver Township
Lawrence County, PA
m: May 13, 1875 in Wurtemburg
Lawrence County, PA
d: May 3, 1924 in Enon Valley
Lawrence County, PA

**John Aughenbaugh**

**Margaret Aughenbaugh**
b: October 2, 1818 in Little Beaver Township
Lawrence County, PA
d: May 30, 1856 in Little Beaver Township
Lawrence County, PA

**Esther Stevenson**

**Clara Rebecca McCown**
b: January 3, 1881 in Little Beaver Township
Lawrence County, PA
d: July 11, 1951 in Enon Valley
Lawrence County, PA

**William Crill**

**Claudia Carmina Crill**
b: December 13, 1854 in Slippery Rock
Mercer County, PA
d: August 14, 1943 in New Castle
Lawrence County, PA
(Almira Home)

**Rebecca Ziegler**

good laugh at the expense of the frustrated fathers!

As I mentioned earlier, Howard and Mamie were close to my cousin Guy and his friend Clif. Howard died in 1946. Shortly after, Mamie moved to California and renewed her friendship with Clif. Later, they returned to Youngstown, Ohio to sell Mamie's belongings, they then returned to California where they married. In addition to selling her home in Youngstown, she also sold Uncle Howard's valuable stamp collection. Eventually she and Clif divorced; but, by that time, her assets were almost nil. Always the optimist—she never complained. She shared her home in Banning, California, with Adolph Baldwin. Adolph, a Navy seabee during WWII, worked as a barber. He suffered from crippling arthritis which he blamed on working in the cold waters of Alaska. Mamie died in a nursing home and was buried in California. Years ago, I bought her half of the lot in Little Beaver Cemetery; and my ashes will be buried beside Uncle Howard.

As earlier mentioned, I was born on the Andrews farm on October 28, 1903 and moved with my parents to Enon Valley in 1904. My father, a Ford dealer, taught me how to drive almost as soon as I was tall enough for my feet to reach the pedals.

My family all grew up in the church, and I became a member when I was twelve. As a child, I participated in all children's and Christmas Sunday School programs. Along the way, I also played the piano for many programs. At one program, I recall a lady harpist, after playing beautifully, commented, "It is strange that so few people learn to play the harp in this world, when so many hope to play the harp in the next world!"

In 1921, I graduated from Enon Valley High School, the only student to matriculate that year and then attended Slippery Rock Normal school. After two years of teacher training, I accepted a teaching position. During the winter of 1922-23, my friend Martha Anderson and I were experiencing our first year of teaching—both in rural schools—with all grades. To get our teaching careers off to a good start, we went via train to Erie, Pennsylvania, to attend the annual teachers' convention. One of the well known speakers attracted our attention with the following comment: "Most teachers feel that their pupils take in our teaching with one ear, let it out the other ear, and keep their mouths open to get a better draft!" At the end of the convention, many of us continued by special train to Niagara Falls. Rooms had been reserved at one of the hotels. Even so, there was no entertainment for New Year's Eve. My friend announced that I could play the piano for dancing. Immediately, tables were pushed aside in the dining room, and a piano was made available. As I played for the dancing, a hat was placed on top of the piano. As couples danced by, coins were dropped in the hat in appreciation for my playing—another warming experience. It wasn't the money that impressed me, rather the thoughtfulness of the dancers.

While attending college and trying to make ends meet during the depression, I continued to teach and also worked at various additional jobs. In the early twenties, I taught seventh and eighth grades in Wampum, Pennsylvania. This school was the only place in my 37 years of teaching where the custodian of the school was also president of the School Board! It was customary there to surprise the teacher with a "fruit shower." On a given day and hour, oranges and apples would roll to the front of the room. Other fruit—a banana, a pear, grapes, plums—were hurriedly placed on my desk. It warms my heart today to think of such fond memories.

I taught grades 5, 6, 7, and 8 in Enon Valley from 1926-30. From 1930 to November, 1942, I taught in Emsworth Elementary, Junior, and Senior High School; and Physical Education from 1938 through mid-November 1942 in Avonworth school.

During my early teaching years, I shared a small apartment with another teacher in the home of an elderly lady. One snowy day, we arrived from school to be met by our landlady with a stack of cold pancakes. We questioned the quality, but she assured us they were good warmed up. We accepted her gift but quietly enjoyed a good laugh. Ella opened our kitchen window and proceeded to sail the cold pancakes out over the covered back yard.    When the snow was gone, there they stood like fortresses, much to our sorrow.

I  received my Bachelor of Science degree in 1937 and taught girls physical education.  In 1941, I received my Masters of Education at the University of Pittsburgh.  In all, I taught a total of thirty-seven years.

*In 1942, I applied to the Women's Army Auxiliary Corps (WAAC),*
*was accepted, and entered military service shortly after Thanksgiving of*
*that year. It was at this time that I started keeping a diary. Part Two*
*contains excerpts from that diary and from letters that I wrote during my*
*time in the WAAC, WAC, and Medical Corp.*

# PART II

## The War Years

## October 1942
### A Running Account of my
### Enlisting in the WAAC

October 26, 1942—mailed my application to the WAAC. They wanted my birth certificate. Because I was born at home, I didn't have such a document. I did, however, find my baptismal certificate which acknowledged my existence and satisfied their need to know that I had been born.

October 30—Had a grand weekend at Na Wak Wa, Pittsburgh's nature camp at Ligonier. When I got home Sunday evening there was a message that I was to report to the WAAC Headquarters in Pittsburgh, Pennsylvania, the next day for a written examination. I called Dr. Floyd, School Superintendent, and made arrangements to be away from my teaching job. Not wanting me to leave, he said, "I hope you fail the test."

When I arrived at the Salvation Army Building where the

examinations were held, there were also seventeen other women. What a test! One hour to answer all one hundred forty-three questions—thirteen pages covering every subject from the Bible to the funnies. While waiting for the test results I had quite a visit with a girl my age who was a nurse. She and I had the highest scores, but her eyes were so bad it was doubtful she would be accepted. I had to return at 4:30 to get fingerprinted and fill out some more questionnaires. We were told to return on Wednesday for our physical exam.

Tuesday morning I told Dr. Floyd that I had another headache for him.

"One more won't make much difference," he replied.

But, when I told him I had passed the written exam, he just wilted. He told me that anyone could be a WAAC and that my teaching job was just as essential as anything I could do in the WAAC's. Of course when I mentioned this at WAAC Headquarters, they definitely didn't agree with Dr. Floyd.

Ella Small, my landlady and good friend, was almost as excited as I was; we were both walking way up in the clouds.

When I reported at 6:00 p.m. on Wednesday evening for the physical examination, there were sixty girls waiting with me. With a last name beginning with "A," I was among the first twelve girls called. We were given long white robes and told to strip. The sleeves were down over my hands. Looked beautiful! First we were X-rayed—three pictures, then weight and height. Next, we were given pretty red corduroy robes with the USA insignia on front. My pulse rate was one hundred and the girl next to me had a pulse rate of one hundred eight. A grouchy doctor growled, "Never take anyone with a pulse over ninety."

"What now?" I asked.

"Never take anyone in the Army with a pulse over ninety," he repeated. Then, smiling, said, "Now, go to the next room—the one marked 'eyes, ears, nose, throat and teeth.' "

We were given a small bottle in which to provide a urine sample. We were in our booths giggling and doing fine when a nurse came along and said, "Okay girls, hold it!" So, Hazel held it! A few minutes later the nurse returned with a tray of cute little white enamel urinals. After passing them out, we giggled some more and gave our samples.

"This is the way we do it in the Army," the next doctor said, sinking a needle in my arm for the Wassermann test. We had been instructed to wear our robes backwards, and this doctor looked us over from the rear to see if our spines were straight and our feet were not flat. My pulse jumped twenty points but he marked it down as eighty. Eye test, same as most eye tests, big "E's" and little "e's."

The doctor in the next room was sitting at a small table. He extended his hand toward me. Thinking that he wanted to shake my hand, I started to extend mine to him, but he only wanted my papers. Looking at me from across the table, he said, with an air of confidence, "Have a seat, young lady. I'm a psychiatrist and I'll be asking you some very personal questions. After looking over my records, he asked, "You're this age and not married yet! Why?" He followed this up with equally personal questions. "Had any children? Have you ever been pregnant? Ever had intercourse?" All these "oh so personal questions," and he never batted an eye as he asked them or listened to my answers.

Then, back to the grouchy doctor. Up to this point the physical examinations had been external or mental, but now that wasn't enough. After completing the exam, he reviewed my records. I was very nervous about my weight. We were allowed only a 16 2/3 percent variance from our stated weight and I was just under the line—164 pounds. Nine of us were through. Six had passed and three were rejected—two for bad eyesight, including the nurse I had met, and one girl because she was too highly emotional. First, I called home, and then I called Tom Small, Ella's husband, and said, "LT. Andrews reporting."

His reply, "Are you starting at the top and working down?"

Friday morning those of us who passed had to return to fill out more forms and be sworn in. While we waited we had a lot of fun talking with a young soldier at the desk. All the forms had F.B.I. headings. Ella bought me a corsage to celebrate the occasion and went with me to the swearing in ceremony. The ceremony was quite impressive. When it was over, I asked the soldier at the desk if there was anything I could show my family and friends that I now belonged to the U.S. Army. At first, he said, "no," but seeing the look of disappointment on my face, hunted around in the desk until he found a small white card. On it he wrote:

**This is to certify that Hazel Viola Andrews has been sworn in as a member of the Women's Army Auxiliary Corps this 6th day of November 1942**

**Signed: Private Burgess**

Before leaving, he told me that I would be called within two or three weeks to report for duty. I hoped it wouldn't be until after Thanksgiving.

I had made plans to visit my sister in Morgantown, West Virginia the weekend of the 14th of November, but at the last minute changed my mind. I had stayed out late Friday night and a wet snow had fallen, so it seemed best to stay home. Then, with this decision made, I thought I might as well place an ad in the paper to try and sell my apartment furnishings. The paper came out about 9:30 that night and ended my plans for a restful weekend. People called until late that night and all day Sunday to say they would be coming over to look at my offerings.

Monday, instead of being rested, I was so tired that I didn't go to school. Must have been fate, because Sergeant Thomas called to tell me to be ready to leave on Sunday, the twenty-ninth of November to begin basic training.

And so began a new and important phase of my life which lasted from 1941-1945. The letters that I have chosen to include in this section of my book provide a very personal glimpse into my life during this time.

# Letter One—My Army Daze

*Sunday, December 6, 1942*
*Barracks E*
*Boomtown, Des Moines*

*Dear Folks,*

*Today marks the anniversary of Pearl Harbor. It also marks the end of my first week as a WAAC.*

*Every morning at 6:35 a.m. we stand reveille, which means we form organized lines of twenty-five girls each. After each group has reported "present or accounted for," we return to our barracks to make up our beds. At 6:45 a.m. we again fall out to march in formation for mess. That's Army talk for food. Today for breakfast we had apricot juice, half a grapefruit, two slices of French toast, raisins, bacon, and coffee or milk—a typical breakfast. On Sundays we don't have to get up until 8:30 a.m. and we don't have to march to the mess hall in formation.*

*Barracks living offers little opportunity for false modesty—your business is everybody's business. So it isn't strange that, within a week's time, one becomes well acquainted with one's barracks buddies. I'm still thankful, proud, and a bit flattered to be counted among those who are in the WAAC.*

WAAC's in Winter Uniform (Hazel 2nd from right rear)

*Of the sixty girls examined in Pittsburgh, I was very conscious of being one of the older ones; however, I no longer have that feeling—there are many grey, even white haired women here who, like myself, have been active in civilian life. The girls are all serious and conscientious as to the motives that prompted them to join the WAAC's. I don't believe one of them, even if she could, would want to return to civilian life.*

*It is now 9:45 p.m. and I am in the latrine seated on the side of a bathtub. Although the lights in the barracks are turned off at 9:45 p.m., they allow us to stay up in the day room and latrines for an additonal hour. The latrine is the place of choice for most of the girls because our day room is in a separate building. After (a) scrubbing the floor in your section of the barracks, (b) doing your personal laundry, (c) laying out your clothes for the following day, (d) shining your shoes, (e) arranging things in the prescribed manner in your foot and wall lockers, you (f) finally, scrubbed yourself.*

*Love,*

*Hazel*

*P.S. Tomorrow I'm on K.P. duty. No! I'm not being punished! All of our duties are rotated and assigned in alphabetical order. That puts me at the head of the list. Ah, me!*

# Letter 2

*Sunday, December 20, 1942*

*Dear Friends,*

*Busy days ahead! I'm the chairman of a committee that is planning a Christmas party for our company of one hundred sixty two officers. Among other things, each barracks will present a skit. Saturday afternoon one of my friends went with me to Des Moines to shop for table decorations, favors, etc.*

*This evening we had a fun get-together in the day room. We sang carols, trimmed the tree and danced. We even danced a Virginia Reel. Refreshments consisted of cocoa and doughnuts.*

*Naturally, I'm not looking forward to celebrating Christmas away from family; however, I'm not complaining because what I'm doing is only a small sacrifice in the big effort.*

*Weather is very cold—snowy and icy. This morning when it was time to fall out for the day, the moon was about to set and the morning star was still high in the sky—a beautiful setting for Christmas week.*

*Two of the many classes we take are of special interest to me—map reading and Army discipline and courtesy. Thursday afternoon we had a one hour lecture presented by a woman officer who, for the next three weeks, will show us movies and lecture on current events. In her first lecture she discussed the events that led up to our current international crisis. She said, "While recent inventions have succeeded in making the world one big neighborhood, we, as yet, have failed to make the*

44

world one big brotherhood." She is right!

The day after Christmas I will be moving out of the Boomtown section of Fort Des Moines. At this time, I still have no idea what my new assignment will be.

When one arrives at Fort Des Moines, the first week is spent in the receiving center—an area better known as the "stables." The stables consist of immense buildings each with at least eight long rows of double-decker bunks. The rows are so long that, if you forget some of your toilet articles when making the walk to the latrine and have to return to get them, you've really had a workout by the time you've completed the second trip.

It is also during the first week that everyone is processed, clothing and equipment is issued, you are taught how to care for your living space or quarters, close order drill is introduced, and you learn how to work and live with others. Also included, in the order of the day, are lectures, Army films and the reading of the Punitive Articles of War. It is the Army's way of acquainting us with Army routine and the information we need to know.

Saturday is moving day—we move to Boomtown, where the training that was started in the first week continues for three more weeks.

The days are never monotonous. If K.P. does not catch up with you during the first week, it is sure to catch up with you eventually. Every day there are countless forms to fill out, examinations, classification questionnaires, and interviews.

Although it is possible to apply for Officer Candidate School right out of basic training, officers discourage doing so. We have been *advised to apply for training in one of the specialist schools and get some firsthand experience on the job before applying for Officer Candidate School. I requested training in either administration or as a cadre. What factors they consider in making their decision, I have no idea.*

*__Later—Flash!__ The orders just came through. Along with five of my friends, I have been selected to go to Cooks and Bakers School. When I joined the WAAC, I had no preconceived notion of what I would be doing; however, I can assure you that I definitely had no dreams of being a cook. My motives for enlisting were unselfish; therefore, I have no intention of protesting about my assignment. If cooks are needed, I'll cook, and furthermore I'll be a good one. I have always enjoyed puttering around the kitchen anyway. Something tells me though, that in the coming weeks, I'll be involved in more than puttering.*

*My new address is: 21st Company, 3rd regiment.*

*Yours for bigger and better mess halls.*

*Hazel*

# Letter 3

*January 12, 1943*

*Dear Friends:*

*The third week of Cook and Bakers School is now underway. We work in shifts. So far my experience in the kitchen has been limited to helping prepare dinner or supper. The hours in the kitchen on the various shifts are as follows:*

|  | Get Up | Go On Duty | Off Duty |
|---|---|---|---|
| Breakfast | 4:00 A.M. | 5:00 A.M. | 8:00 A.M. |
| Dinner | 6:30 A.M. | 7:30 A.M. | 1:00 P.M. |
| Supper | 7:30 A.M. | 12:30 P.M. | When kitchen & dining rooms are immaculate— usually 7:00 to 7:30 P.M. |

*Pastry, meat, frozen foods, vitamins and field cookery are among the cooking arts included in our daily lectures. When we report to our assigned Mess we check the posted roster to find out what our assignment for the day will be—pastry, butcher, vegetables, range, or dining room orderly.*

Hazel in Cook's Uniform

Yesterday I was assigned to work pastry with another girl. Our assignment—to make oatmeal cookies. I did the mixing while she weighed and measured the ingredients. I was really "in the dough" all afternoon. We used ten pounds of flour, four pounds six ounces of lard, one dozen eggs, and other ingredients in like proportion. After mixing, we rolled the dough in balls and stacked them, pyramid style, on a large work table. Just before baking, we flattened the balls on cookie trays. Recipe yield—nine hundred cookies.

Pushing Cart Filled With Rations

*My first job as butcher, which, by the way, was my first day in the kitchen, included the skinning and slicing of a beef liver so large it almost covered the butcher's block. That chore was followed by slicing sides of bacon. Our training also includes practical experience in preparing food without benefit of modern kitchen gadgetry. In a field kitchen this training would be important. My rural upbringing came in handy here, as well as in the dressing of chickens, and the boning and rolling lamb for roasting. The preparation of meat is followed by a thorough cleaning of the butcher block—wire brush and all.*

*Assignment of vegetables might include peeling seventy-five to one-hundred pounds of potatoes and removing any eyes or spots by hand with a paring knife. The peeling and dicing of ten pounds of onions is another possible task as is the preparation of fresh vegetables for salads.*

*Last evening I completed my second assignment as first cook. Our main dish was chili con carne. I'm assigned to what is considered a small mess hall; yet, even here, we had three 6 x 18 x 36" ration pans filled with chilli. We also served peas, wedges of lettuce with French dressing, baked custard, milk, coffee, and bread and butter. The average size mess seats 375, but in our largest mess we can serve as many as three thousand at a meal.*

*Although the cooking is done on gas ranges, the dining area is heated with four coal stoves. Each kitchen has four gas ranges and a steam table. It is the responsibility of the dining room orderly to keep the fires in these coal stoves burning. Carrying in the coal and carrying out the ashes are also necessary evils—*

50

as are setting up the tables and scrubbing the cement floors in the kitchen and dining room.

It remains true that the one thing you can count on in the Army is change. Every week some girls complete their training and move out of our barracks to be replaced almost immediately by others moving in to take their places. Under ordinary circumstances we would be strangers but here, we quickly become one big happy family. Only last night we got some new girls in our barracks. One girl, whom I knew from working with her in the mess hall, moved into the lower bunk to my left about 9:20 p.m. When she arrived I had just finished washing my hair, but I hurried to help her make up her bunk before the lights were turned out. As I helped her, she told me she was celebrating her twenty second birthday. She is a former beauty operator. She calls me Andy.

Another new girl came in quite late, long after lights were out. Hurrying to make her bed up in the dark, she wrenched her shoulder. Although we had never met, I got out of bed and massaged her neck and shoulder. She proceeded to call me Mom.

Four gigs have been charged against me. Two for having a poorly made bed—the cover wasn't stretched and tucked in tightly enough. A shoe, not in perfect alignment with its mate, accounts for my third gig. The fourth I got for neglecting to initial my name on the gig sheet. No justice!

We're suffering through the coldest weather of the winter so far; however, in spite of the bad weather, plenty of warm clothing, bedding, quarters and good food are keeping us fit.

*Many of you have written to suggest that, in giving up a good teaching job, even though it's only for the duration, that I'm making a sacrifice. In all sincerity, I must tell you that the education I have received in the WAAC is superior to much that I have received in civilian life. Furthermore, whether I return to the classroom or go on to some other occupation, I will be a much broader and more understanding person because of what I have learned here.*

*The friends I have made come from varied backgrounds—one of my best friends worked in a government printing office in Washington, D. C., while another owned a beauty shop in Chillicothe, Ohio. One older woman in my barracks is a grandmother who, in her younger years, as a dancer, traveled from coast to coast in a popular New York theatrical production. The girl who borrows my Pittsburgh Post Gazette each day to keep abreast of sports news was a professional baseball and basketball player. One of the girls in our mess hall is a professional trapeze performer. Just rubbing elbows with so many people of different professions has broadened my horizons.*

*Our chief evening diversion is to buy a big bag of popcorn, go to a movie, and really enjoy ourselves. When working the supper shift we go to the 7:30 movie directly from the mess hall wearing our white or blue iniforms to the show. Can you imagine cooks in uniform and white hats going to the movie houses at home being accepted? The same type of dress can be seen on Sunday at the church services.*

*8:00 p.m., Saturday,*
*January 16*

*The mess halls are inspected several times every day and, once a week, a plaque is awarded to the mess hall considered to be the cleanest and best managed. During my first week in Cooks and Bakers our mess hall received the plaque and, as a reward, each of us was given a day off.*

*I'm enjoying my vacation, or, as we call it, "leave." I am staying in a home with rooms for tourists that was recommended to me by the local Chamber of Commerce. Those of you who know how much I enjoy my solitude can appreciate how much I am enjoying these twenty hours away from my sixty roommates.*

*Before coming to town this afternoon I learned that our mess hall, Mess #4, has, once again, been selected as the Honor Mess which means I'll be getting another extra day off soon.*

*It's funny but the hurdle-jumping I had feared so much before coming to the Fort has never materialized; in fact, I've not even seen a hurdle—thank goodness!*

*I've concluded that I can write longer letters and more interesting ones by writing only once a month. I shall call this letter number three. If you want to continue on the present list of correspondents, please answer soon. I do enjoy writing, but I also like to receive letters.*

*Many of you know that, whenever I eat out, I have developed a habit of looking for trade names on the china. At the cafe in Des Moines where I ate this evening, the china was*

*"Mayer" china from Beaver Falls, PA. Many of the coffee mugs in our mess halls are labeled "Shenango" from New Castle, Pennsylvania.*

*I will be completing my six weeks training in Cooks and Bakers School on February 5th. After that, I'm not even wagering a guess as to where I'll be or what I'll be doing, However, I'll try to get another letter on the way as soon as I find out.*

*I hope you'll all forgive me for not including a personal note to each of you. Time is precious.*

*Yours for victory,*

*Aux. Hazel V. Andrews*

## Letter 4

*January 31, 1943*

*Dear Friends:*

*You would really enjoy the sights here in the barracks this evening. One of the girls, a pre-law and student of psychology, is interpreting handwriting for several of the girls. Directly across the aisle from my bed, a former beautician is trying to study. Some girls on the upper bunks are sitting cross-legged as they write letters while two or three other groups are sitting around talking. And, above all this, the*

*Eversharp radio program is playing full blast.*

*All through Cooks and Bakers School one of my really good friends has been Alice, from Kansas. She recently received her B.S. Degree in education but chose to become a WAAC rather than teach, at least for the time being.*

*The other evening some of my buddies came into the barracks and told us that Olivia Borden, the former movie actress, was working in their mess—she even served on K.P. duty. The cooks speak very highly of her general attitude and sincerity of purpose. She has now completed her basic training.*

*One day last week I talked with a woman on K.P. duty, a French war bride from World War I who married an American soldier. The mother of five children, one of her sons has been in the Army Air Corps for almost two years. Her youngest child is now sixteen. Her husband is on active duty and she left their farm in Utah to serve in the WAAC.*

*Following up on my last letter: Marie, the thirty-nine year old grandmother, who was once a ballet dancer, is now in Officer Candidate School. May, the former baseball player has been transferred to another position on the post. Oh, and we have another former professional baseball and basketball player—her name is Florence and she's from Cleveland, Ohio.*

*As student cooks, we have little to do with the meal planning; however, in our daily classes, we do receive instructions on this subject and are encouraged to make suggestions for varying the menus. Ideas for making use of leftovers are particularly welcome. There is no food wasted in the kitchens; for example, most of the meat is boned before cooking and the bones are then used as the source of stock for our soup.*

*The mess officer, with the assistance of the mess sergeant, makes out the menus. Individual mess halls, according to the supplies and leftovers they have on hand, may alter the menus somewhat. In other words, all of our mess halls basically serve the same main dishes on the same day. Food conservation may be fairly new to civilians, but not to the Army. They have been doing it for a long time.*

*This morning, I started working the breakfast shift. Got up at and was on duty in Mess #4 by 5:00 a.m. That sounds like a terrible hour to be getting up. And it is! However, it is worth it because we are done by 8:00 a.m. and, other than one hour of close order drill after dinner, we are free for the rest of the day.*

*This morning I was first cook. The main dish was pancakes. We use two big griddles, each holding as many as thirteen pancakes at one time. Flipping them at just the right time to keep them from burning keeps one on the ball They were good.*

*Today was a day to try one's heart and soul! Our class, the 17th, is now the oldest in the barracks. Many of the cooks from previous classes have been moved into different barracks. We had grown pretty well acquainted in recent weeks so, as they descended the stairs with their luggage, such admonitions as "Make the cooking good!" and "See you over there!" were spiritedly called out to them.*

*A number of you have asked if the discipline is strict and if I feel completely regimented. Frankly, I don't feel that I am under any stricter discipline here than that which was imposed on me in college. Of course, pride in the uniform may have some influence on my attitude. I would consider it a serious offense to disgrace the uniform. Even in the Army one's superiors are human and I feel we are treated as such.*

*Stockie, the girl from Akron who was my buddy during basic training, is now attending radio school in St. Louis. She writes that, even though they work long hours, in many ways they lead the life of Riley. Her letter to me was printed, not written, because radio operators must be able to print at a rate of twenty-five words per minute. It's not easy—try it.*

### *Wednesday, February 10*

*Because of general changes being made in the schools, our training did not end until Thursday, February 9th. The next day I reported to the consolidated mess to work. Consolidated is the large mess—the one that serves three thousand persons a meal. I assisted in preparing sixteen hundred pounds of potatoes, cracking thirty-six dozen eggs for meat loaf, and helping to dice sixty pounds of cheese which was to be used to make sauce for cauliflower.*

*Instead of the ten and fifteen gallon boilers we used in Mess 4, here we use steam-heated, steel-jacketed vats of sixty or eighty gallons capacity and, instead of spoons, wooden paddles are used to keep things stirred.*

*The butchering and pastry baking is done by the night shift. Every other day I report to work at 5:00 a.m. and stay until 1:00 p.m. On the other days I go on duty at 10:45 a.m and then work until 7:00 p.m. Although I no longer have to attend classes, it is my hope to receive some additional training before going into the field. Two possibilities exist for more training but, since they are both so indefinite, I won't try to tell you about them at this time.*

*For several days now the weather has been spring-like. The air is quite balmy, but we're obliged to keep our feet on the ground. I really should say __in__ the ground—the recent thaw has loosened this Iowa gumbo no end. Cleaning one's galoshes under running water with a scrub brush is routine following each trip outdoors.*

*Following the last heavy snow we were issued good old fashioned four-buckle arctics to supplement our two button rubber galoshes. The arctics serve to give one better lifting power and a broader base to offset the tendency to sink.*

*Our shoes, by the way, include two pairs of good substantial oxfords plus one pair of above-ankle laced shoes—like men's shoes. Ah, me!*

*February 13, 1943*

*Now that the weather has moderated somewhat, we have been doing some drilling out of doors. The girls in basic training are getting more, of course. It isn't unusual to see a dog running along beside a unit of girls in formation, ears high and barking merrily. The sudden changes in direction shouted by the instructor as they drill, really confuses everybody.*

*A big review honoring Mrs. Franklin D. Roosevelt and Mrs. Oveta Culp Hobby is scheduled for tomorrow. Since the weather has been so severe, this will be the first big review since I arrived. Unfortunately, I'm scheduled to be working in the consolidated mess where the honored guests will eat and won't get to see it. Need-*

*less to say, we've been preparing for this event for days. I even cleaned the stove pipes with steel-wool and cleanser.*

*This is without doubt a country of free speech. From the range to the butcher's block, our daily discussions include such subjects as politics, cooking methods, romance, weather, and finances. Never a dull moment, and what a lot of fun.*

*February 14, 1943*

*As anticipated, Mrs. Roosevelt and the other guests arrived yesterday before the noon meal and inspected both the kitchen and the immense refrigerator. They were so close to me, I could have reached out and touched them when they walked by. We were all wearing spotless uniforms, aprons, and caps.*

*The two tables we had set up for the guests and their party looked somewhat out of character with tablecloths, daffodil centerpieces, engraved silverware, and crystal.*

*They were in the mess hall for almost two hours. Many little incidents added to the day, of course. Later, while we were eating, Director Hobby came over to thank us for preparing such an excellent dinner. To say that we were thrilled is putting it mildly.*

*Our kitchen duties kept us busy for the rest of the afternoon; however, we did take time out to watch several companies march by on their way to the parade grounds. The air was quite chilly but clear for such a celebration. Hearing the martial music from the nearby parade grounds added to the thrill and excitement of the day.*

*I am imposing on some of my friends to*

help me with the heavy work of mimeograph-
ing these letters. You may note that there is no
change of address on the envelope. There is
nothing definite along that line to report at this
time.

My notes from day to day are very incom-
plete and I know I have omitted some things I
intended to include. However, there will be
another day. So . . .

*Yours for victory,*

*Hazel*

*February 27, 1943*

P.S. Even though our class finished Cooks
and Bakers School on February 9th, I continued to work in the consolidated mess until the
20th when I received my assignment to Officer
Candidate School. This is a very intense six-
week course. After that, I will be a 3rd Officer.
(I hope). One week of Officers' Candidate
School is now over. There will be no time for
letter-writing during the coming weeks. However, reading letters, you know, helps to bolster
the soldiers morale.

*Approved by Public Relations*
*Hazel V. Andrews O. C*
*5th Co. 1st Regt.*
*U. S. Army Post Branch*
*Fort Des Moines*

# Letter 5

**Autography of Hazel Viola Andrews
The first part of this autobiography
was begun just after my enlistment
in the WAAC in 1942**

*During our first week of school we were
required to write our autobiography. The following is a copy of the one I wrote for this assignment:*

Thirty-nine years ago, on October 28, 1903, I, Hazel Viola
Andrews, first saw the light of day. I was born in the same farm
house and in the same room in which my father was born twenty
seven years earlier. Then, when I was one year old, the family
moved to Enon Valley, Pennsylvania. Soon afterwards a baby
boy arrived. That completed the family—Ruth, my older sister,
myself, and Arthur, our younger brother.

### My School Life at Home

The most outstanding event in my elementary school life was
no doubt the result of an extreme swing of the education pendu-
lum. The new fifth-grade teacher attempted to make me right-
handed. This autobiography is being written with my left hand.

Our local high school felt the effects of World War I and,
when I graduated in 1921, I had the distinction of being Valedic-
torian and Salutatorian. Sad to relate, I was in the lowest fifth. I
graduated alone!

### On My Own—Away at School

At the end of one year at the nearest State Normal School,
Slippery Rock, Pennsylvania, I returned to Enon Valley to teach

61

in a nearby school. Following my second year at Slippery Rock, I accepted a teaching position at Wampum, Pennsylvania—seventh and eighth grades.

The fall of 1926, I returned to Enon Valley to teach grades five, six, seven and eight in the borough schools. My pupils, since they all knew me, addressed me as Miss Hazel rather than Miss Andrews.

In May of 1930, having been elected to teach the middle grades at Emsworth, a suburb of Pittsburgh, Pennsylvania, I received my last salary check from my home town. I signed a contract for $1,400.00 with Emsworth.

Two years at Slippery Rock and seven years of teaching preceded my arrival in Emsworth in the fall of 1930. I was fortunate to have moved shortly after the stock market crash in 1929 and before the ensuing depression.

In mentally reviewing those early years in Emsworth several things come to mind. The economy went from bad to worse and, the following year, our salaries were cut by ten percent. Within the next year or two special teachers Marie Ruffing (music) and Miss Miller (art) were dismissed. Also the school year was shortened. Many teachers, to supplement their salaries, had to search for summer employment.

Until I received my Bachelor of Science degree from Pennsylvania State College in 1937 and my Masters degree from the University of Pittsburgh in 1941, I spent many, many evenings, Saturdays and summers pursuing those ends.

In the spring of 1938 the adjoining boroughs of Emsworth and Ben Avon formed a union school district. When the new superintendent arrived, one of the vacancies was that of girls physical education teacher. I was fortunate to be named to fill that position. Since then, I have been a full-time teacher of physical education in the Avenworth schools—junior high school girls in Emsworth—junior and senior high school girls in Ben Avon. My work has included teaching intramural sports for girls and working with the girls in various sports clubs.

During Christmas vacation of 1941, I attended forty-five hours of concentrated Red Cross first aid instruction to certify as an instructor. During the ensuing weeks all of my girls in the Junior Red Cross Club received the standard course of instruction.

### My Summers or my Peaces and Cream

My father, a Ford car dealer for twenty three years. taught me to drive almost as soon as I was tall enough for my feet to reach the pedals of a Model T. Dad maintained the only taxi service and, at that time, the laws governing a driver's age were quite lax . Most of the time, Arthur and I were the drivers. My father was of a very generous nature, and if a car was available it was "at the mercy" of his kids. Until I bought my first Ford in 1924—a 1919 model coup—I didn't realize that gasoline cost money!

My parents recognized that I had a natural ear for music so, for a good many summers, I took piano lessons. I have never regretted what, at the time, I considered a major imposition. For many years, before going to the city to teach, I played the piano at the Presbyterian church where Dad directed the choir and Mom supported the alto section.

The way in which I have spent my summers has been controlled by either an obligation to my position or by financial pressure and an adventuresome spirit. In obligation to my position, the summers of 1930, '31, '32, '36, '37 and '41 were spent in school while the following years fall under the category of financial pressure and an adventuresome spirit:

1926—Waited tables at the Carey—a resort hotel in Chautauqua, New York.

1927-1928—Gave piano lessons—often receiving eggs, strawberries, raspberries, and other goods as payment.

1929—Made auto trip to West Virginia via Chicago, Illinois.

1932—I made nine trips driving my car to Chicago to the World's Fair called "The Century of Progress." Each of my four passengers paid me $12.00 apiece for the round trip. We left on Monday and returned on Saturday. I made very little money, but had a wonderful time.

1933—I took three fellow teachers on a 10,400 mile tour to the West Coast. In accordance with our agreement of one and one quarter cents per mile, each of my four passengers paid me five dollars every four-hundred miles—enough to pay for the gas and for my trip as well.

1934—I made three trips to our glorious Northeastern United States and to Montreal and Quebec. Again, each of my three passengers paid me 1-1/4 cents per mile for the trip.

1935—I sold my car to concentrate on completing work for my B.S. in Education at Penn State where tuition costs five dollars a credit.

1936—Christmas vacation. Enjoyed a trip to Florida—this time as a passenger instead of the driver.

1937—I achieved my goal and received a Bachelor of Science degree from Slippery Rock.

An interesting sidelight: When I had no car and wanted to go home to Enon Valley for the weekend, I would take the train. But, I would have to call the Pennsylvania Train Station in Pittsburgh on Friday and make arrangements for them to stop the Chicago to Pittsburgh passenger train #118 at Enon to pick me up for the return trip on Sunday afternoon. They did this for me several times.

1938-1939—Helen Creese (Pluchel) and I rented a furnished cottage at Madison-On-The-Lake and took in summer boarders. The second summer Ann Agnew and Pat Giovengo went with us to help with daily chores. We had a great time.

1941—I Received my M.S. in Education and Physical Education.

1942—I worked as a waitress at The Flanders, a fashionable hotel in Ocean City, New Jersey. That fall was the first year I started teaching with money in my pocket.

In November I enlisted as a Private in the WAAC. A mistake in the eyes of many of my friends who felt that I had just reached the point where I should sit back and rest on my educational laurels. They failed to realize that my spirit would never adhere to such a program.

# Letter 6

*Wednesday,*
*March 31, 1943*
*Service Club Lounge*
*Fort Des Moines*

*Dear Friends:*

*For the past week, while waiting for my orders to come through, I have been sharing a barracks with two-hundred and eighty other women. The majority of these girls, just like myself, have just completed basic training and will be transferred within the next few days.*

*Every week, as the result of being eliminated by the screening board, approximately twenty girls arrive here from an Officer Candidate Company. Others come because they were eliminated during the last week of Officer Candidate School by the very aptly named "Murder Board."*

*Eighteen of us were washed out of Officer Candidate School Company one week ago today by the Screening Board. Today, the Murder Board is in session for the rest of our company. Being the victim of such a board is scarcely my idea of fun. In all probability, another fifteen or so from my former company will be joining us here before the end of the day.*

*Applying for Officer Candidate School involves a formal application, a written recommendation from one's former company commander, and the successful completion of many examinations, interviews, questionnaires, and the all important interview with the First Officer Candidate Board.*

*The purpose of this board is to draw a candidate into conversation and ask leading questions so they can better judge the capabilities of the candidate. To serve as a WAAC officer, a candidate must also measure up in areas other than formal education. It's true: "Many are called, but few are chosen." My orders came through and I moved into the Officer Candidate barracks on February 19th. Classes started on Washington's Birthday. What a thrill it was to begin on the anniversary of our first president's birthday. We were surely a happy company, divided the usual way—three platoons of fifty girls each.*

*At the end of the third week we received*

*individual reports of our academic standing. Mine was satisfactory.*

*In the middle of the fifth week, the screening board passes judgment. It is the good fortune of some to complete training without ever encountering either this or the Murder Board. However, such was not my luck.*

*From the first day of training on, we were told that we would be watched closely during the entire period. The WAAC is looking for leaders. Giving the impression of being a good potential leader among one hundred fifty picked leaders calls forth one's greatest efforts. Until I was called before the Screening Board I had no reason to believe that my efforts weren't on a par with the other women in my company. However, during noon break on Wednesday of :the fifth week, nineteen of us were called before the board and told that we had been eliminated as potential officers. We were given one hour in which to pack our belongings and move into the "Stable" and await further orders.*

*Before leaving home, I knew that there would probably be times when I would question why I had given up the security of a job to go into the Army. The seventy-two hours following this sudden turn of events was one of these times.*

*It would have been bad enough to be drowning in one's sorrow, humiliation, disillusionment, and disappointment in solitude, but to be with so many others who were also experiencing the same heartbreak, was genuine adversity. In spite of my strong negative feelings of crushing defeat, I, along with some others, attended the movie on post that night. Although the colorful, tropical picture was indeed beautiful, I can still recall the warm tears of disappointment that were streaming down my cheeks while watching the picture. The privacy of the darkened movie house lent the opportunity to vent to my feelings.*

*During the next several days they kept us so busy there was no time for us to lick our wounds. In fact, I felt as though salt had been poured on mine. The first day I was put on K.P. The second day I was assigned to work as a janitor in the very classroom where I had attended class. Since we were still in the midst of Iowa muddy gumbo, this day's toil couldn't have been more degrading.*

*It is not "ours to reason why." Suffice it to say that, of the thirty-four that were washed out by the boards, twenty-eight of us are thirty years of age or older. I suppose that, in the long run, one could say that those of us who are older and have faced some of the grim realities of life, can better face up to such an experience. Of course, some persons go through life without facing a challenge. Like my American forbearers, I, too, enlisted for an uncertain future; now, philosophically, I am trying to face that future.*

*Until new orders come through, my daily work continues at the consolidated mess. My free time shall be employed in reading, writing, movies and anything else I can think of for distraction from my thoughts. Certainly raking over cold ashes will not renew the fire.*

*Please accept this letter as a factual account. I hope to bounce back soon and will continue to give an honest account—wherever and in whatever capacity I'm asked to serve.*

*Yours for Victory,*

*Hazel.*

*ADDENDUM* I wrote the following letter to Ede Brungard, following my dismissal from Officer Candidate School. Ede is a fellow teacher from Emsworth, Pennsylvania.

*Dear Ede:*

> *Wednesday afternoon eighteen of us were called into the Orderly Room and told to remain in the barracks. After the rest of our company left for afternoon class we were told we had washed out of Officer Candidate School and were given one hour in which to pack our belongings and leave the barracks. Some of us managed to get a moment with our Platoon Lieutenant to inquire why we had failed. I was told by my Lieutenant that I lacked forcefulness. Interpret that as you may.*
>
> *Among my fellow "washouts" is a newspaper woman from California, a graduate of the University of Oregon, a teacher from Oklahoma, a graduate of the University of Oklahoma, a girl with an M.E. degree from New York University, a girl who had been in charge of the educational exhibits at the Museum of Arts and Sciences in Rochester, N.Y., a girl who gave up a $3,000 Civil Service job in Washington, D.C., and another who had, prior to enlistment, been in charge of Airport and Airway Control at a prominent western airport—and many other college graduates— all just as outstanding in their particular field.*
>
> *Since we are not considered good material to be officers, some of are back doing K.P., while others have been assigned to clean classrooms. The same classrooms where only yesterday we sat in as Officer Candidates. I'm on*

*the verge of being bitter. Here we have all of these highly trained women and how are we being used—to peel potatoes and push a broom and mop.*

*We have been told that within the next few days we will be moved away from the post. Because I went through Cooks and Bakers School I'll probably be assigned as a cook. I hate the thought of that. It seems strange to feel that way since the days I spent in Cooks and Bakers School have been among my happiest days so far.*

*A few weeks ago I was afraid I would be shipped out before making Officer Candidate School and now, given the chance, I have failed to meet the challenge.*

*One of my instructors in the Cooks and Bakers School, a home economist who also failed to make the grade, is now in Mess Sergeants School. I hope that I, too, am assigned as some kind of Sergeant or cadre.*

*During the past several weeks my study has been so intensive—something that I won't miss and don't want any more of for a while. In Officer's Candidate School we were made conscious, 24 hours a day, that we were potential officers. Readjusting from that point of view is not easy. One of the things that hurts me the most is measuring the abilities of those who remain in training and no doubt will be commissioned. Granted, I don't have a voice like a worker in a boiler factory and, in civilian life, never used force to get things done; however, I feel I have more friends that respect me for that very reason. This is the first time I have ever questioned the value of character and good breeding. There is so much I could write to you, but until I establish a more stable mental*

70

*equilibrium this will have to suffice.*

*I don't want sympathy! I have had disappointments before and come through smiling. The less you write to tell me your reactions to this the better I'll like it. I am not trying to hide or cover up that I have failed, nor am I attempting to hide or cover up the fact that apple-polishing takes people places! When I am permanently located, I'll drop you a card. In the meantime, my address is 1st. Company, 3rd Regiment.*

*Feel free to share this letter with anyone you wish. Outside of personal letters to my immediate family, this is the only one I am writing. You might let Ella know, as well as the gang.*

*Yours for Victory,*

*Hazel*

# Letter 7

*May 18, 1943*
*69 WAAC Post Hq. Co.*
*Fort Custer, Michigan*

*Dear Friends:*

*It is now more than a month since I arrived here. Again—the only thing constant in the Army is change. Just as in civilian life, the happiness and satisfaction that one enjoys is measured by one's ability to adjust. At times, however, this is difficult, since, in the Army, the changes are unpredictable and uncontrollable.*

**Arriving at Ft. Custer, Michigan**

*In civilian life you can take a job, estab-
lish roots and, if you do a good job, anticipate
promotion. Here, the philosophy is, "don't think
of tomorrow—do the best job you can and get
all the happiness you can today." What has
been a part of your Army life is no indication
as to what your future service may be.*

*May 30th will mark the start of my sev-
enth month in the Army. I've learned so much
in such a short period of time—basic training,
Cooks and Bakers School, several weeks in
Officer Candidate School, mail orderly, and
now, apprentice physical therapist.*

*Since my last letter I have gained more in-
sight into the Army, but less understanding. I've
come up with a simple philosophy that I'm trying to live by: "By the inch—life's a cinch. By
the yard—life is hard." Before Officer Candidate School was completed thirty-four of us
were either removed or reassigned, and are now
scattered in camps throughout the country. I
could write a book about my experiences in,
and reactions to, that school.*

*Though the WAAC is only one year old, a
number of traditions have been established—
traditions that add color to our routine. Among
these traditions is the story of the goldfish.
Some months ago one of the Officer Candidate
companies acquired some goldfish; however,
when the company graduated and was commissioned the fish had to be disposed of. Graduation morning, the girls in the company, taking
the goldfish with them, went en masse to the
barracks of the girls who would be the next to
graduate. Since then, this has come to be a
tradition every graduation  morning to deliver
the goldfish to a new home.*

*It is said that good luck will come to the*

*officer who, upon being saluted for the first time after receiving her bars, gives a dollar to the person who salutes them. I understand that this tradition is practiced in other branches of the armed services. I know of one girl who boasts about receiving eight dollars.*

*It was just a week ago that I returned from a ten-day furlough. It was so good to get home. Although in the past I had spent short periods of time away from home—five straight months without seeing anyone from home was different. My furlough came through so quickly there was little time to plan. I did most of my travelling at night so that my days would be free for visiting.*

*Among the highlights of my furlough was visiting with relatives and friends, attending church, parties, club meetings, and visiting school. And, with assistance from mother nature I, once again, experienced the feelings of rejuvenation by such simple springtime offerings as sassafras tea, horse radish, asparagus and rhubarb. Seeing the beauty of the wild flowers—the violets, dog tooth violets, and trillium—brought back memories of my childhood joys.*

*On the return trip to the base I arrived in Detroit early Monday and planned to spend the day resting there. I had even arranged through Traveler's Aid for sleeping quarters at the U.S.O. dormitory for service women. When I arrived at the dormitory at the Y.W.C.A., I found that some of the girls staying there were in the Canadian Women's Corps. Instead of resting, we spent the day seeing the sights of Detroit. We even had our picture taken in a five and dime store basement so we could exchange them. The day served as a fitting finale to my furlough.*

It was fun to go home, but now it was
good to be back on the job where there is much
work to be done.

Life here at Fort Custer is, in many ways,
similar to life at Fort Des Moines. We keep
much the same hours but, instead of attending
classes most of the day, we now have a job to
do. The hospital serves the military and civilian personnel stationed at Fort Custer. A truck
transports us to and from the hospital every
morning and takes us back to our barracks in
the evening. There are about fifty of us working in various departments throughout the hospital. The messenger girls knew they were doing a great deal of walking but, until they carried a pedometer, we weren't very sympathetic
to their complaints of weariness. One of the
girls walked over twelve miles and another
more than nine miles.

It is possible that my assignment may be
changed again. On the other hand, I won't be
at all surprised if I'm stationed here for the duration. You can see why I've adopted the philosophy I have.

In one of my first letters to you I wrote how
the girls come from every part of the country.
It's something we take for granted. Now that
we are far removed from civilian life and clothes
we have to resort to other means to identify
each other. Visualize twelve girls dressed iden-
tically and then try to describe one in such a
way that she will be recognized from the other
eleven. Very difficult to do!

Some weeks ago I listened in on a conversation among a group of girls that contained
such tidbits as: "In civilian life what kind of

*clothes did you wear? Did you wear tailored or dressy clothes? What colors did you prefer?"*

*Pets are numerous around the post. The 35th WAAC Post Headquarters Company that has been stationed here since mid-January has a cat named K.P. We now have a dog that we call Mickey.*

*In Michigan, spring seems to take a long time to arrive. We are still having many rainy, disagreeable days—quite a contrast to the weather back home when I was on furlough. It is still too cold to wear cotton uniforms, even if we had them.*

*On Sunday, our two WAAC companies were taken by special train to participate in the "I Am An American Day" celebration in Detroit. After arriving here on Thursday, April 8th we paraded in Chicago on Saturday of the same week. This was our second time away from Fort Custer.*

*Loretta Young will be visiting the base today and tomorrow. We were quite thrilled to learn that she would be eating in our mess hall. She ate the main course with the 35th Company and, along with her Military Police escort, had dessert with us. Afterwards, she went outdoors so the girls could have their picture taken with her. She is both beautiful and charming.*

*Somehow, this letter doesn't seem as spontaneous as some of my previous ones.*

*Yours for Victory,*

*Hazel*

*P.S.—The poems that follow were received*

*from some of our boys. They are self-explana-*
*tory. I'm sure that the thoughts expressed in*
*them will call forth memories to all ex-WAAC*
*personnel.*

I left my lovely tropic isle,
Where the sun is bright and flowers smile.
Where palm trees kiss the fragrant breeze,
And the skies reflect the cobalt seas.
Where the moon comes up like a golden ball,
And mango trees grow straight and tall.
Where you play all day and dream at night of past,
Where rum is only a buck a quart,
And friends drop in for a friendly snort.
Where bananas and melons grow all year,
And you wallow in servants up to your ear.
Oh, it's really a life of lazy ease,
A paradise with you holding the keys.

As I said before, I left my isle,
To come to the states for a deed worthwhile.
In other words, to join the WAAC's,
To do my duty—get down to facts.
In no time at all I was called to account,
For my mental state—were my tonsils out?
Were my feet both mates, did my shoulders sag,
Did I walk like a woman or droop like a rag?
Were my teeth my own—did the right leg kick,
When the doc hit my knees with his little old stick?

Were my eyes O.K.—was my nose on right,
Did I love my mother—could I fly a kite?
Was I subject to colds and coughs and sneezes,
Could I hold my own with the winter breezes?
After all this ended I was sent away,
To come back again some other day.
Well, I waited and waited and watched the mails,

Tearing my hair and gnawing my nails.
Till one day it finally came,
The letter to lead me to glory and fame.
I packed my bag with gusto and glee,
And hopped on a train to my destiny.
The first thing I noticed as I rode along,
Was the change in the weather, could I really be wrong?
Or was that stuff snow that came drifting in clouds,
Obscuring the scenery with ghostly white shrouds?
It was snow all right as I learned very soon,
When the train finally stopped in the early forenoon.
I was there at last—in far famed Des Moines,
Where zero is nothing in weather or coins.

The first thing I did was lift my own bag,
Into a truck with a grim Army tag.
I slipped and I skidded—I fell with a thud,
In the Iowa concoction of ice, snow and mud.
I rode with a dozen or more other girls,
All dressed to the teeth and their hair all in curls.
We darn near froze on our way to the post,
And I couldn't quite figure where I hurt the most.
I got out of that truck just like I got in,
With my feet in the air and the ground on my chin.
I carried that bag from here over to there,
And slipped once again to make everything square.
My eyes they were running, my nose it was red,
And I knew that I was in for a cold in the head.
We went into some kind of a barn or a hall,
And everyone sat in her own little stall.

Until she was called by the doctor who said,
Stick out your tongue if there's one in your head.
We all then reported to a place called the "Stables,"
Some two hundred strong with our cases and labels.
Before we could sit, we had to make bunks,
And start into cleaning out the lockers and trunks.
By then it was time to get ready to dine,

Our mess, I should say, and a mess was our line.
We straggled along like poor wandering sheep,
And I straggled along too with nary a peep.
We filed into mess and were given a tray,
With separate compartments for oats and for hay.
A huge drinking mug without any handle,
The way that I held it was really a scandal.
From then on till dark we were dashing like fiends,
And then came the call to wash out latrines.
When nine-thirty came I laid down with a groan,
Thinking sadly of a beautyrest mattress and home.
So soon fell into a sweet slumber sound,
When the darn whistle raised me up with a round.
Hitting my head on that upper damn bunk,
With a crack plainly heard all the way to Squeedunk.
That day was memorable in more ways than one,
But the one main event with its place in the sun.
Was the issuing of coats, galoshes and hats,
And for a moment I thought I was bats.
Instead of the smart overcoats I had seen,
On all of the WAAC's on the movie house screens.
We were given some outfits that didn't make sense,
And made us all look like walking pup-tents.

From then on we marched and we cleaned and drilled,
And at some time each day our poor minds were filled.
With punitive articles of war and such things,
As A.W.O.L. and the sorrow it brings.
We learned to about face, to right face and then,
We fell out on the double to start in again.
Well, just as things were beginning to shape,
We were given our shots and boy did they take:
Smallpox, tetanus and typhoid, by golly,
And the ensuing night was not very jolly.
When we at last had settled down into a groove,
Learned when to stand and when we could move.
The news went out through the barracks like mad,
It was "Boomtown" for us and all that we had.

79

And boomtown it was after a long weary walk,
Of all of ten minutes by somebody's clock.
And rehashing things that we already knew,
We started to school like children once more.
We learned about who, why and where was the war.
We went to the movies to learn how to drill,
We learned to make beds with questionable skill.
We also learned about K.P., and gee,
When it's washing those pots—do they have to call me?
It's G.I. for this and C.Q. for that,
It's B.G. and T.A. and who swiped my hat?
To top it all off, there's formal inspection,
And where to hide things calls for serious reflection.
But of course there's a place it's become quite a gag,
It's a famous spot under the old barracks bag.
In spite of all of this and our hours of pain,
There's something we all wish to make very plain:
Our hats are all off to our officers here,
They're doing a swell job and deserve a big cheer.
So, until we are sent on to some other place,
We'll all hang together as we freeze hands and face.
We'll work and we'll clean and we'll never grow lax,
Here's to God bless Our Country, and God bless the
WAAC's!

Author Unknown


## Where

Somewhere in the Pacific where the sun is like a curse;
And each long day is followed by another slightly worse;
Where the coral dust blows thicker than the shifting desert sands;
And the white man dreams and wishes for distant fairer lands.
Somewhere in the Pacific, where a girl is never seen;
Where the sky is never cloudy and the grass is always green;
Where the rats' nightly prowling rob a man of sleep;
Where there isn't any whiskey and there's no beer to be cheap.

Somewhere in the Pacific where the nights were made for love;
Where the moon is not a slouch; and the southern cross above
Sparkles like a diamond in a balmy tropic night;
It's a shameless waste of beauty when there's not a girl in sight!

Somewhere in the Pacific, where the mail is always late,
A Christmas card in April is considered up-to-date;
Where we never have a payday and we never get a cent,
But we never mind the money for we'd never get it spent.

Somewhere in the Pacific where the ants and lizards play;
And a hundred fresh mosquitoes replace each one you slay;
So take me back to Frisco, let me hear the mission bell,
For this Godforsaken outpost is a substitute for hell!

Author Unknown

# Letter 8

*October, 1943*
*Co. B - 4621 S.U. WAC Det.*
*Fort Custer, Michigan*

*Dear Friends:*

*I have written only one letter since arriving here in the early part of April. There are several reasons for this. When I was new to the Army, unexpected happenings warranted a place on paper. But now I know that in the Army the unexpected is really commonplace. I used to jot down notes to be rewritten later in letter form but have discontinued this practice.*
*Probably the most practical reason for my*

*delay in writing is that my work in physical therapy, where massage and exercise are the order of the day, is so exhausting. I am the only woman technician in our physical therapy staff of seven. Another WAC serves as the office clerk in the department.*

*Our staff represents a good cross-section of America. The head of our department, a sergeant, comes from Michigan and is a graduate mortician who comes from a family of funeral directors. Our other sergeant is a male nurse who eventually hopes to become a doctor. The corporal, an American-born Japanese, is very intelligent and looks forward to the day when he can return to his wife. He enlisted long before Pearl Harbor. Another member of our department is a big Jewish fellow who formerly was in the leather goods and luggage business. A day never passes that he doesn't say, "I want this war to get over so that I can go home." He writes faithfully to his wife every day. I tease him and tell him that they probably put him in physical therapy because he knows his hides and therefore, should be highly qualified to massage. Then we have a fiery little Italian who is so unpredictable in his conversation he adds sparkle to the day for the patients. Many times I could be embarrassed, but it is much easier to pretend I am hard of hearing or that I don't understand. The WAC clerk is the youngest in our group and did similar secretarial work in civilian life.*

*Bonnie, one of my barracks buddies and bunk mate, is from the deep south. After making friends with the proprietor of a Greek restaurant and his wife in Battle Creek, Bonnie and I were invited to visit them in their home.*

82

*Over peach brandy, Bonnie divulged that she had been married three times. Her first husband was a full blooded Indian. Her second turned out to be a bigamist. Her third and present husband, about twenty years her junior, is serving in the Merchant Marine. Hearing this, our hostess guilelessly inquired, "Gracious, Bonnie, what did you do with the second one—kill him?" Bonnie laughing, responded, "Well, I wouldn't say that I did and I wouldn't say that I didn't."*

*Bonnie, like myself, is an older WAC. She remembers how, after World War I, she was unable to find work. She is now anxious to become a cook because she theorizes that, even in a depression, people still must eat. Her theory is if she is a good cook it will assure her of three square meals a day.*

*On September 1st I was promoted to corporal. Remember in my last letter how I told you that in the Army one must learn to live and enjoy today and forget about tomorrow. Well, I'm frequently reminded that I'm not doing that very gracefully. The number of promotions and the rate at which they are distributed has been affected by our change in name from WAAC to WAC.*

*By the way my promotion came through on a Saturday. There was little time to sew on my new corporal stripes before going into the Battle Creek Hospital so, thinking it would not be noticed, I went with my new stripes sewn on only one arm. I'll never try that again—almost every patient asked me, "Were you made corporal on just one arm."*

*I've found myself. I enjoy my work very much and can't think of another job I would prefer to this one.*

*The area around the hospital is strictly rural. Marie, a farm girl from North Dakota, and I have been taking a stroll every day during our noon break to drink in October's bright blue weather. We enjoy each others company and the beautiful fall foliage and recite seasonal poetry as we walk.*

*Even though I am one of the oldest WAC's in our company; yet, some of my best friends, Mildred and Florine, are among the youngest: Mildred is from Texas and loves country music. Florine, a tall brunette from Oklahoma, joined the WAC when her twin sister eloped.*

*In the middle of August, because of the death of my grandmother, I was granted another furlough and returned home . Had she lived until December, she would have been eighty nine. Mother was the only girl in a family of six children. My sister, Ruth, also came home for the funeral and we had a nice visit.*

*When the WAAC became WAC, we were all given an option to leave the service. I seriously considered getting out. In fact, I had three long talks with my company commander about it. My reasons were purely selfish. After all, it wasn't selfish motives that had prompted me to enlist in the first place. I have lived long enough to know that there will always be personal disappointments to overcome. Here, though, it is a matter of judgment rather than problem solving.*

*Our barracks are similar to the men's barracks. In fact, the buildings in all the company areas are arranged the same, street after street. On one occasion, a slightly inebriated soldier mistook our barracks for his. We told him, in no uncertain terms, that he was in the wrong barracks. Strangely enough, all those female voices had a somewhat sobering effect on him.*

*Our day begins at 6:00 a.m. Reveille is at 6:25 a.m. and is followed by either drill or physical training. Before marching to breakfast we are dismissed briefly to police the area. Even though there are ample G.I. cans provided for the disposal of candy papers, cigarette butts,*

WAC Formation, Ft. Custer

85

match stems, coke bottles and such, one can always find some around. With so many hands picking up, it is surprising what a short time it takes and how quickly many of us gravitate to the furnace room in the back of the barracks—especially if it is a cold morning.

After breakfast we have approximately one-half hour to put our house in order and make the laundry room, tubs, bowls, and latrines presentable.

At the end of the day, one of the major interests is to inspect the gig sheet. Every day our Commanding Officer inspects the barracks. The gig sheet registers her findings. Even after all these months, someone will still occasionally overlook some part of the morning detail. Being charged with four gigs in a week calls for special detail.

The two rooms comprising our day room are now attractively furnished thanks to the generosity of The Infants Service Group, a Jewish organization in Detroit. We now have two lovely sofas, six upholstered chairs, two glass-topped coffee tables, lamps and end tables to add to our comfort! Some weeks ago, on a Sunday, we entertained the members of this organization so we could thank them in person and they could see firsthand the results of their generosity. Menus are the same at all mess halls. A little item of special interest—the main dish that day was ham.

I usually spend some of my free time in the hospital library. A book I am presently enjoying reading is Ted Malone's, **Pack Up Your Troubles.** I like it because it was written to appeal to people in the service. I'm also enjoying reading such poems as Rudyard Kipling's **If**, Samuel Foss', **The House By The Side Of The**

***Road***, *Carl Sandburg's **The People, Yes**, and Don Blanding's **"Vagabond House."***

*Until last week our company had the privilege of going to the mess hall for a bed time snack. If there were no appealing leftovers in the refrigerators, there was always bread, butter, jelly and peanut butter. Many of us took advantage of that privilege. But now all that has changed and there will be no more lunching between meals or bedtime snacks. Thursday evening Florine and I went to the mess hall to retrieve our wash board. Once we were inside we couldn't resist the opportunity or the temptation to pick up some eatables. We're still laughing about our stealthy return to the barracks with cake, tomatoes, oranges and a cantaloupe. The problem was to find a place of safety from the officers and other girls who would insist on sharing our booty. After casing out all the possible areas, we finally decided on the furnace room where we sat and enjoyed our snack in the dark.*

*We now have our own beauty shop. Two girls who had been beauticians in civilian life were assigned to run the shop. I doubt that their assignment to this work was the glamorous position they had pictured they would have in Army life. Their equipment is modern and the girls do good work. Today, during my afternoon break from K.P., I had a shampoo and set. Yes I am still doing K.P. Regardless of rank, every girl in the company has her turn. Even though we are not feeding a full company, the work still includes washing the dishes, pots and pans, scrubbing the tables and benches, and cleaning the garbage pails and grease trap. One's first thought at the end of a K.P. day is a hot shower and some fresh air.*

*In planning for long winter evenings in the barracks I've decided to use this letter to do a little advertising for something I would like so much to have—a small workable radio. They are so hard to find, not only for those in the service but for civilians as well.*

*We get food both in the WAC mess hall and at the hospital. As a result, we eat too much. About two weeks ago I decided to stop eating my noon meal at the hospital because that was easier to do than resisting all the in-between meal snacks. On my way to the Red Cross library, I usually stop at the WAC ward to visit with any of the girls who happen to be patients. Then, at the library, I scan the current magazines and newspapers. **The Ernie Pyle column** holds special appeal for me. On October 2nd, **The Saturday Evening Post** carried a good article about his career. I also enjoyed an article in **Look Magazine** written by Leland Stowe entitled, **Why Aren't More American Women in Our Fighting Forces?***

*Some of us have bought season tickets to attend the Kalamazoo Civic Players series. Of course we will have to go the Army way—by truck. **Claudia** is to be their first presentation. Another diversion we have is bowling. At least twenty of us bowl on a regular basis.*

*One day last week we were ordered to report to our day room at 6:00 p.m. for a meeting. It seems that one of the officers had looked over our area and concluded that it needed some extra policing. After returning to our barracks to don fatigue slacks, we went outside to meticulously police the grounds. While we were there, a battalion of soldiers marched by. As they passed where we were working, their drill sergeant gave the order to, "Whistle* cadence." This consisted of "One, two, whistle, whistle." Of course, they were doing it for our benefit. At the first pause in their cadence we began to howl, wolf style, drowning out their whistle cadence. We laughed and laughed. This little friendly exchange put a different light on the extra work we were doing.

Hilda, from Akron, Ohio, who I met in basic training, is now stationed at Kellog Field near Fort Custer and is learning how to operate a Link Trainer.

As previously mentioned, when we changed from WAAC to WAC, we had the option of being discharged from the service. Many of the cooks took advantage of the opportunity and elected to be discharged. As a result the cooks that are left have to work long hours and extra hard. To give them a rest, last Sunday I asked to go into the kitchen and relieve one of the cooks for a day. With only one other cook we did all the cooking for the day. Many of the girls were surprised to find out that I had been through Cooks and Bakers School. Although I enjoyed the change of work, I'm still happy to be in physical therapy.

Today, as usual, Marie and I went for a long walk during our lunch break. At about the halfway point in our walk we dropped to the ground under a Maple tree and, using our gas masks as pillows, enjoyed the bright, blue October sky.

This afternoon the Physical Therapy Department is being fumigated. Confidentially, I think it is no mere accident that today is also the second game of the World Series. Have been sitting at a table on the lawn of the hospital since 1:00 p.m. writing, reading poetry, visiting with patients, studying humanity at large.

*At the end of a weary day nothing revives me more than responding to "mail call" and finding two or three newsletters from home.*

*Yours for Victory,*

*Hazel*

# Letter 9

**December, 1943**
**Madison, Wisconsin**
**Christmas Letter**

*Dear Friends:*

*The job of addressing envelopes and tagging one hundred and thirty 1944 calendars is just completed; but, it wasn't an entirely unpleasant task, since it brought to mind so many pleasant memories. There must be something of the elephant in me—I can't forget! Most of you I can associate with very happy times. I say most of you because a few of you I have never met; however, your interest in the cause of the WAC has made you my friend.*

*Friday, for the first time, I ran into someone I had known before entering the service— Barbara Browne from Emsworth. At noon, when I came out of the Hospital for lunch, I ran into her. Barbara had been a student of* mine in grade school and also in her senior year of high school. Since her graduation from the Pennsylvania College for Women two years ago, she has been working as a chemist in Madison. We made plans to meet again.

On October 14th, I received orders saying that I was to report to the University of Wisconsin Medical School in Madison and attend their school for Physical Therapy Technicians. Sixteen of us are now sharing a mixture of Army and college life. We travel to and from classes together, eat together, sleep together, and study together. Because we are all following the same course of study, from the college standpoint, it is a rather unusual situation.

Two similar classes are also in progress, one is at the University of Pittsburgh with eighteen WACs, and the other is at Stanford University in California with seventeen members.

Like all Army specialized training programs ours is a concentrated intensive course. Also, in order to complete the six months course by April 18th, we must attend class eight hours a day, six days a week. That means we are in class from 8:00 a.m. until 5:20 p.m. Then, in addition to the time spent in class, we have at least two hours of compulsory study time every evening except Saturday. We have a 1:00 a.m. bed check on Saturday night, on other nights it is 10:30 p.m.

This course is so intensive that we sometimes come from class feeling completely snowed under. Just learning the medical terminology is a major accomplishment in itself. My studies in college provided me with some knowledge of the human body, but I really hadn't realized until now how little I knew. Before coming here, I hadn't even knocked at the door of science.

91

Madison WI Home During PT Training

Classroom Instruction U. of W.

*One of my hardest battles during the past year has been reconciling my reasoning to actual circumstances. In my last letter I boasted about finally learning how to enjoy today, forget about yesterday, and not anticipate tomorrow. That habit has almost proved my undoing*

93

*in trying to master anatomy, physiology, hydro-therapy, asepsis, sterile technique, massage, and various heat and ray lamps. Many more courses will be introduced as we complete these. Gradually we are getting acquainted with the clinics in the various hospitals that are connected with the University.*

*In our group are girls from New Jersey, Oregon, New Mexico, Texas, Iowa, Washington, Minnesota, Florida, Kentucky, and one who lives in Alaska. A few weeks ago I bought a United States map and posted it on the living room wall. On it we have labeled our home towns, alma maters, and the locations of our previous Army assignments. Three of us are from Pennsylvania.*

*Margaret Warren, our first Lieutenant, is living with us and, from the Army standpoint, is looking out for our interests.*

*Dr. Francis E. Hellebrandt, head of the Physical Therapy Department, is responsible for the planning and expediting of the course. We all sense the months of work that had to have been put forth by her to make our program function so efficiently and marvel at her energy and enthusiasm. Our instructors include heads of departments—the best the University has to offer. I only hope we can rise to the goal that has been set for us.*

*Ours is the first WAC contingent to be part of the university. The women from the Navy, the WAVES, have been here for more than a year. Their last radio class will leave here next week. During our first week here we met them when we were all in formation. They sang a little ditty entitled,* **We're Never Too Busy To Say Hello.** *All of us sing quite frequently when in formation and crossing the campus.*

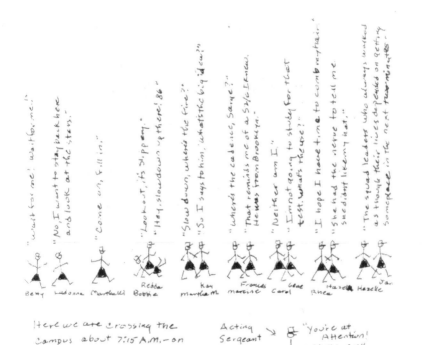

"Wait for me! Wait for me!"

"No, I want to stay back here and look at the stars."

"Come on, fill in."

"Look out, it's slippery."
"Hey, slow down up there! 86."

"Slow down, where's the fire?"
"So I says to him, what's the big idea?"

"Where's the cadence, Sarge?"
"That reminds me of a style I knew. He was from Brooklyn."

"Neither am I."
"I'm not going to study for that test, what's the use?"

"I hope I have time to comb my hair."
"She had the nerve to tell me she didn't like my hat."

"The squad leaders who always worked as though their lives depended on getting someplace in the next few minutes."

Betty   Ladonna   Marshall   Rebda   Kay   Frances   Gene   Hazel   Jan
                              Bobbie  Martha M  Martine  Carol  Rhea  Hazele

Here we are crossing the campus about 7:15 A.M.—on our way to breakfast and subsequent classes.
Credit for the artistry goes to Ladonna — our stargazer.

Acting Sergeant

"You're at Attention! Hut 2, 3, 4" (These remarks are lost in the general confusion)

Janet

## Stick Drawing at U. of W.

*At the end of six months our formal train-ing will end and we will be assigned to various Army hospitals to work as physical therapy apprentices for the next three months. Then, upon completion of our apprenticeship, we will be discharged from the WAC and become a part of the Army Medical Corps.*

*There is a possibility that, at some time during our training, we may get a seven day furlough. We're all very hopeful that we will because, after only two months here, we are feel-ing the strain of all work and no play.*

*We will not have to attend classes on Christmas day. That will be our only holiday vacation; but, I'm not complaining. If I can successfully pass the registry examination of the American Medical Association and serve in an Army Hospital, I will be happy. After the dura-tion it might even become my new profession.*

*Thanks for the many letters you have sent and the holiday greetings. I am enjoying every single one. It is very doubtful that I will have the time to write another letter during the ensu-ing four months.*

*Early in our training one of our instruc-tors quoted Emerson—"**Struggle is the essence of growth.**" I frequently repeat that quote to myself and the other girls. We agree that we should come through this course as Big people.*

*The best of a happy holiday to you all!*

*Hazel Andrews*

# Letter 10

*Saturday, February 27, 1944*

*4654 S.U. - A.S.T.P. - W.A.C.*
*717 Langdon Street*
*Madison, Wisconsin*

Dear Friends:

For the past two weeks I have had to resort to postcards to keep my family informed.
The closer we come to completing our physical
therapy course, the more each minute counts.
Our course officially ends on April 8th; however, we are slated to take the registry exam of
the American Medical Association on April 1st.
We are still hoping that we will get furloughs,
but still don't know for sure if we will get them
or whether we will be ordered to report directly
to an Army hospital to begin our three months
apprenticeship.

In writing these letters I usually apolo-
gize to the WAC proofreaders that help me for
the lack of unity, coherence, and emphasis in
what I have written. One of the girls reminded
me that I am writing to my friends who don't
rewrite and reorganize the letters they write to
me. Accepting that attitude will possibly account for more grammatical errors than usual.

Ours is the only WAC group on the campus and our uniform sets us in a world apart
from others. Early on in our training we were

97

*looked upon as shining examples; however, our instructors soon learned that, even though we were in uniform, we were no different than the other students and needed the same discipline to motivate us. After all, we are only uniformed products of the same school systems as the other students. I shall never forget a remark made by Kay after our instructors discovered this. She said, "I believe they have discovered that we are mortal." She has a very quick wit.*

*Most of us don't even want to think of that day in July when, for the last time, we will take off our WAC uniform and don the uniform of the Army Medical Corps as a physical therapy aid. Even though most of us have done our fair share of griping about the WAC, we still reminisce with a feeling of nostalgia about our experiences as a part of Corps. Bobbie, talking to me about physical therapy, said, "We're not just on the ground floor, we **are** the ground floor!" And, you know, she is right!*

*Because our course of training is not open to WAC officers, many of them envy us this opportunity. One officer friend, in writing to me at Christmas, said, "I understand that your course is a killer-diller; however, it will be the thing when the war is over."*

*Our time is so completely planned that we don't see a great deal of Lieutenant Warren, the WAC officer assigned to look after us. Being responsible for sixteen of us girls didn't keep her very busy so she has found a niche for herself in Dr. Hellebrandt's office where her previous training in typing and shorthand is being put to good use. She may envy our opportunity to take this course, but we envy her having the opportunity of working so closely with Dr. Hellebrandt.*

*Referring back to Christmas: After collecting a stack of Christmas cards I taped them to the wall of my room in the form of a Christmas tree. I thought it was a good idea but, like pine needles, the cards wouldn't stay put. At night, I would be just about to doze off when swish—another card would break loose and glide across the bare floor to land near my gifts on the floor under my Christmas tree. My tree of cards lasted just two nights.*

*Christmas vacation was short and, because we were excused from evening study for three nights, most refreshing. ChristmasEve most of us went to the midnight church service. This was preceded by a choice of hiking, ice skating, or listening to the opera in front of an open fire. I chose to join the hikers. We got lost trying to hike around Lake Wingra. It was after dark before we came out on a road and caught a bus to get us back to our group.*

*On Christmas day we were entertained— Christmas dinner and all—by Dr. Hellebrandt in her beautiful home. We surely did justice to a delicious meal of cold sliced turkey, cranberry sauce, and all the other good things she had prepared.*

*Dr. Hellebrandt had traveled extensively through Europe with her sister where she bought many of her beautiful china dishes. After dinner we sprawled on the floor before the open fireplace within easy reach of an immense platter of homemade cookies. It was truly an evening of good fellowship and a day I will long remember.*

*The day after Christmas I spent in Madison at the home of Lieutenant Colonel and Mrs. Oscar Wallace, formerly of Emsworth and Avalon, Pennsylvania. Mrs. Wallace and I* attended the same church in Emsworth and enjoyed reminiscing about the people and places back home. I couldn't help but feel conscious that I, a lowly corporal, was sharing the day with a colonel and his wife. A most unusual situation but a truly delightful day.

Last Sunday I visited the Wallace's again and Mrs. Wallace took me on a tour of Truax Field where her husband is stationed. It gave me an unusual feeling to see all the enlisted men saluting us as we drove by.

Today, Saturday, the 15th of January, marks the halfway point in our training. Since returning from Christmas break we have been cramming in preparation for mid-term tests. The exams started at 8:00 a.m. After completing the tests we waited in a dither until Miss Kohli, Dr. Hellebrandt's technical advisor, came out at 5:00 p.m. and handed each a sealed envelope. Most of us went to our rooms to ponder the contents in private. Each envelope contained a composite grade and a personal note from Dr. Hellebrandt. Later, most of us shared the contents with one another and agreed that she knew us better than we knew ourselves. In fact, one girl remarked, "She hit me right between the eyes." Oh! By the way, we all passed!

Living so close together is like being part of a big family. And, like every family, we may have our differences and quickly forget them. In arguments within our group, we may take sides; however, if someone outside the group says something unkindly about one of us, we bond together and come to her support in a hurry.

In recent weeks our training included twenty hours of surgical observation. From glass enclosed balconies above the operating *room we witnessed a great variety of operations. The drama of an actual operation is much more impressive than the movies depict. I was impressed by the care with which all those concerned practiced sterile technique, the precision with which the surgeon handled the many different instruments, the agility with which the nurses assisted and kept an accurate account of all the sponges and instruments used, and the skill and devotion of the anesthetist. I would risk my life with one of these operating teams any day. During these operations the surgeons would, for our benefit, comment on their findings and the progress of the operation.*

*Each week finds us putting more and more hours in actual clinical practice. Among the techniques we are applying are hydrotherapy, which includes many different types of baths for the treatment of various diseases. One type of treatment, that I had only heard of before, was the wax bath. It goes without saying that it is used only in treating arms and legs.*

*Our instruction includes many hours in the theory and practice of the Kenny Technique for the treatment of infantile paralysis. Then, of course, we have different lamps using dry heat, ultra violet, infrared, luminous heat, short wave diathermy, and others.*

*Believe it or not, styles even change in the wearing of our WAC uniform. Since arriving in Madison we have been allowed to wear our neckties out when we are not wearing a blouse. Formerly, we had to tuck them inside our shirt front. We can now wear the strap diagonally across our body instead of letting it hang from the left shoulder. The third change came this weekend when brass buttons replaced the olive drab buttons on our blouses and overcoat.*

*By the way, there are nineteen buttons on the overcoat.*

*This has not been a typical Wisconsin winter. Prior to arriving here we had all heard many stories about the severe winters; yet, back home in western Pennsylvania, we would consider this to be a very mild winter.*

*Our possibilities for fun are limited. For anatomy and therapeutic exercise, four of us have been reviewing our muscles together. A stranger, seeing us sitting around on the floor in our pajamas with one bare foot extended, wiggling our toes and working those little foot muscles for all we're worth, would wonder about our sanity. The shout of glee that follows isolating a particular muscle is where the fun comes in.*

*After our evening meal, we usually get back to our barracks around 6:00 p.m. Within an hour the majority of us are bathed, have our hair "up" for the night, our washing done, and are ready to relax.*

*Next week we have five more final exams scheduled which means I won't have a minute to spare. So—I shall bring this letter to a close. I hope to hear from many of you before we bid farewell to Madison in early April. However, any letters addressed to me at the Enon Valley address will be forwarded.*

*We are expecting Major Vogal, the head of physical therapy for the entire U.S. Medical Corps to be visiting here over the weekend of March 4th. We keep thinking that next week can't possibly be busier than this one, but it usually is! There seems to be no rest along the way.*

*The Army moves in strange ways and one learns to accept consequences without grief.*

*We have all made some good friends among the teaching staff as well as among our classmates; yet, knowing that many of us will never meet again, we keep counting the days until we leave. This move means that, for the sixth time, I will have to start all over again the process of making new friends.*

*More than once, one of our instructors has referred to life as, "this veil of tears." I, however, would rather accept the philosophy of Dr. Hellebrandt, who exhibits her feelings every time she says, "We're beautifully and wonderfully made."*

*Yours for Victory,*

*Hazel V. Andrews*

# LETTER 11

10 June 1944
WAC Detachment
Valley Forge General Hospital
Phoenixville, Pennsylvania

*Dear Friends:*

*Letter writing serves as a good excuse for me to record on paper events which I might otherwise forget. Even in a letter of this length, it is impossible to write about all the interesting events and impressions that happen every day.*

*Saturday, April 7th, found sixteen of us boarding trains leaving Madison and the University of Wisconsin for new assignments—four* to the West Coast, one to Texas, two to Indiana and the rest of us to general hospitals here in the East.

Dr. Hellebrandt's final message to us sealed for all time our final stamp of approval of her. In her message she emphasized that the University of Wisconsin has always encouraged individuals, free thinkers and, as she so aptly put it, "queer eggs and rare birds." She was right! Students of all kinds have always found a warm welcome on the Wisconsin campus.

The Army, on the other hand, has little tolerance for the individual and tries, in so many ways, to level individual initiative and thinking. Our Army basic training had accomplished that goal and had molded us into fairly uniform subjects. Then, with little warning, we were thrown into the contrasting environment of the university. Dr. Hellebrandt gave us credit for surviving such a contrasting situation in a truly commendable manner. Confidentially, I think that before the six months were over, even the teaching staff may have considered us to be among the "queer eggs and rare birds."

One year after passing through the Chicago train station on my way to Fort Custer and my first WAC assignment, I passed that way again enroute to my new assignment at the Valley Forge General Hospital. During the two hour layover in Chicago, I had a glorious visit with three girls from the Fort Custer WAC detachment who were spending Easter weekend in Chicago. Our furloughs hadn't come through so I had no time off before reporting to my new duty station. I stayed awake until 2:00 a.m. Easter morning to see the lights of Enon Valley as we rushed through on the train.

Two of our three months apprenticeship are

104

*now over. I can't think of another section of the country where I would rather be than right here. The red brick hospital buildings are all new and we are within one hour traveling distance to the weekend attractions of Philadelphia, New York, and Washington.*

*It is fun to be living in a WAC barracks again. Every Tuesday and Thursday we get up at 5:30 a.m. and have to be ready for drill by 6:00; the other mornings we get to sleep in until 6:30. Our working day starts at 8:00 a.m. and ends at 5:00 p.m. with one hour off for lunch. Even though we can't be out past 1:30 a.m., it is wonderful to have our evenings free. However, after an honest day's work, our bunks are too inviting to take advantage of that privilege. We have no Sunday work.*

*Carol Ferguson of Wrangel, Alaska and Hazelle Erickson of Minneapolis, Minnesota, came here with me from Wisconsin. In addition, there are three WAC apprentices from the physical therapy class at the University of Pittsburgh, and four civilian girls who are serving their apprenticeship here. The girls from the Pittsburgh class are Betty Wood of New Jersey, Imogene Speegle of Alabama and Helen Matchett of Washington, D.C. They are very fine girls.*

*I must mention the event and advent of the bicycle! Our first week here Carol and I placed an advertisement for bicycles in a Philadelphia newspaper. The following Sunday, a rainy day, was spent in closing the deals. We brought the bikes back to Phoenixville on the train and then rode them from the train station to the barracks.*

105

Soldiers at Valley Forge G. H.

*Enumerating the events of that day would make for a long story—suffice it to say that Carol has done much more riding than I. Riding a bicycle is definitely not a means of satisfying one's requirements for rest.*

*The Easter season was an ideal time to arrive here. We have observed spring and summer develop from their earliest signs to a colorful, warm reality. For Hazelle and I this is euphoria. We have both served on several Army posts and can see that there is much work to be done here. We both feel that we are doing a good job and would be quite happy to stay here for the duration.*

*Marion Hipple, from the WAC detachment at Fort Custer, lives near here and recently came home on a furlough. We got together twice while she was home and reminisced about our days at Fort Custer. On one of those occasions she invited me to dinner at her aunt's home in Phoenixville. After dinner, they drove me out to Valley Forge Park to see the dogwoods—the blooms were at the height of their beauty. The contrast of an occasional pink dogwood against the background of the many white ones was awe inspiring. They were so beautiful! The following evening I persuaded two other girls to return with me to view them again. We managed by hook and crook—and I do mean crook—to make the trip; however, we felt we were amply repaid for all our efforts.*

*Many other things besides receiving treatment adds to the color of our patient's lives. For example, one of the girls in our barracks recently returned from a furlough only to learn to her sorrow that, during her absence, her boyfriend had met someone else. The following Saturday morning while applying her makeup and getting ready for work she was*

107

*humming, "Will I ever find the boy in my mind, the one who is my ideal?"* It was probably just coincidence and doesn't mean a thing, but one of the first patients to come into the clinic that morning was singing, *"In my arms, in my arms, ain't I ever going to hold a girl in my arms!"* Later that morning one of our blind patients, came in whistling, *"A pretty girl is like a melody."* When I told him about the other tunes I had heard, he laughingly remarked, "Sounds like those two ought to get together."

You may have read recently of the generous gift that was given by Mr. Bernard Baruch to promote research in physical medicine. The committee directing this research is under the leadership of Dr. Lyman Wilber of Stanford University. They have defined "Physical Medicine" as, "The use of light, heat, water, cold, electricity, message, manipulation exercise, spas, climatology and hydrology; the latter specializing in baths, sprays, and the like." In addition to investigating the present methods of treatment in physical therapy, research is also being done in the fields of osteopathy, chiropractic and naturopathy.

Many treatments are very simple but are also very important because a lack of knowledge as to when and how to apply even a simple treatment can result in a permanent handicap.

Because the healing process is more or less unpredictable, our work is never monotonous. We get a great deal of satisfaction in seeing improvement in our patients.

A few weeks ago one soldier, home from camp on furlough, was brought here in a wheelchair with the right side of his face completely paralyzed. After treatment, which included both heat and facial exercise, he has recovered complete *function of his facial muscles. Part of his therapy, between treatments, was to chew and whistle. I told him that I was sure that there were many patients who envied him that prescription.*

*One soldier, who was having heat applied to his back to relieve pain, fell asleep while holding pictures of his little three-year-old daughter in his hand. The scene was so touching, we took turns tiptoeing into the room to look.*

*There is another soldier who has been in the hospital for many, many months receiving treatment for an upper arm injury that severed the nerves controlling the back of his hand. Recently we have been seeing a weak muscle contraction—a sign that his muscles are starting to function again. To say that he is overjoyed at this recent progress, no matter how small, is putting it mildly.*

*Another patient, a lieutenant, enjoys reading Shakespeare while exercising his foot in the whirlpool bath and while exercising on the apparatus in the gym. While this is serious reading, the most popular reading material among the patients is comic books.*

*One afternoon, a young colonel, reporting for treatment of his leg injury in the whirlpool bath, asked if he could remove his pants rather than just roll the pantlegs up. Before I could return from my trip "through channels" with an answer to his question, he had removed his trousers and proceeded with the treatment. There he was, sitting there in his gaily colored shorts, nonchalantly reviewing a song he was composing. Later, I remarked that it was probably that very type of decisive action that was responsible for his being a colonel at such a* young age. He certainly didn't stand on ceremony and definitely believes in cutting through all the unnecessary red tape. Oh, by the way, the answer which I brought back to him even though it was a bit late was "No!"

A blind patient, also an officer, was in a particularly jovial mood the other day. In addition to being blind, he has lost both hands and most of his forearms. In the course of his treatment he asked, "Have I told you about my accident?"

"No Captain, you haven't!"

"Well," he responded with a smile, "my mother tried to break me of biting my nails when I was a child—this is the result."

Laughing, the technician replied, "Well you surely went to town that time, didn't you!"

The attitude of these patients is typical and should serve as an object lesson to those of us who mercifully have been spared the actual hands-on reality of this horrible war.

Some fleeting impressions of people and places: Our first weekend in New York included travel by subway, elevated, double-decker bus, taxi, and the Staten Island Ferry. It also included a meander through the old Trinity Church yard near the battery and reading epitaphs on tombstones—including Alexander Hamilton's. We took a walk down Wall Street and a trip up to the cloisters. Several generous-hearted civilians gave us a lift in their cars. We inspected and admired the grandeur of the old Reed Mansion which is being used as a Women's Military Service Center. We even ate in an automat and visited the Stork Club!

Churches visited in New York: St. Patrick's Cathedral, The Little Church Around the Corner, and the oldest Dutch Reformed Church in

*America—St. Thomas' Episcopal and Marble
Collegiate Church—where we heard the noted
Dr. Norman Vincent Peale speak. He is a very
inspiring speaker. Following the service, we
enjoyed a luncheon that the church provided
for those who are in the military service. I
visited Mr. and Mrs. Harold Brinig, formerly
from Ben Avon. Mrs. Brinig is the Chairman
of the Hostess Committee for Service people.*

*In Washington, a former fellow teacher,
Mrs. P. J. Stupka, entertained us in her most
attractively decorated home. Hazelle and I
enjoyed it no-end. Our sight-seeing included
a tour of the Capitol, National Art Gallery,
the Washington Monument, a trip across the
Potomac to the Pentagon Building, and a ride
around the Lincoln Memorial.*

*Major Vogel, the head of physical
therapy for the entire Army Medical Corps,
who visited us in Madison during the latter
part of our theoretical training, also came to
visit us here. Last Thursday she observed us
as we treated patients and later talked to us
as a group where she encouraged us to main-
tain the "Human Touch." Giving treatment is
not only physical but also psychological. Re-
covery from a severe illness or injury is never
a purely mechanical process. A very vital part
of our responsibility is to know our patients
and encourage them to fully cooperate in carrying out their prescribed treatment. I hope
we may live up to the high ideals she set for
us.*

*In addition to providing general treat-
ment, Army hospitals also specialize in spe-
cific treatments. And here at Valley Forge we
specialize in treating blind patients and those
who require plastic surgery. An article in the*

*May 6th edition of the **Saturday Evening Post**, tells of the plastic surgery provided by our hospital.*

*It may sound as though we spend a lot of time traveling and, I must admit, we are taking advantage of our location. But remember, prior to this assignment, we had not been away from home for the entire six months we were in Madison. And, if we can get away and relax on the weekend, I believe that we can provide better treatment for our patients. We are enjoying it while we can. Who knows, it may not be too long before we may be assigned duties beyond reach of these cities and other things American.*

*At home I always enjoyed rearranging furniture; however, in this rambling construction, which I call a letter, I'm not attempting to dust or polish any paragraphs, much less rearrange them.*

*We are still hopeful that we will be granted a furlough before our scheduled move in early July. In addition to looking forward to a visit home, we feel the need of a good rest. In the meantime, keep your letters coming. They provide a refreshing diversion.*

> *Yours for Victory,*
> *Hazel V. Andrews*

*P.S.—All is quiet again between my WAC neighbor and her soldier boyfriend. This evening I heard her singing, **"When your heart goes bumpety-bump, it's love, love, love."***

FLASH ! FLASH ! FLASH !

*From midnight on Saturday, July 8th, until*

*8:30 Sunday morning we will be civilians. After that, we will officially be physical therapists in the Medical Corps and entitled to wear the uniform of an Army nurse. Following that date and a ten-day delay enroute, my new address will be:*

*Lieutenant. Hazel V. Andrews P.T.A.*
*c/o Nurses Quarters*
*Halloran General Hospital*
*Staten Island, N.Y.*

## Letter 12

*17 December, 1944*
*Halloran General Hospital*
*Staten Island, New York*

*Dear Friends:*

*The nearer I come to being an actual participant in the war, the more difficult writing becomes. It isn't a lack of interesting experiences that has delayed the completion of this, my 12th letter, for my work is quite interesting. It's just that we are kept so very busy*

*Halloran is a very big hospital. A current movie short which you may have seen at your local theater, includes some fine shots of our department. Generally speaking, this is an evacuation hospital; however, many patients are held here for definitive treatment. The number of patients treated daily is fairly constant. This constant coming and going of patients is carried on so efficiently many of us are not even conscious of its happening.*

*At the present time we have seven physical therapists in our department and six WAC's who provide able assistance. Since coming here, I have been treating patients on the wards who, for whatever reason, are unable to come to the clinic. It would be difficult to find a more outspoken or democratic group of men. For example, one patient boasted that he was in no hurry to get out of bed—that he might stay in bed until the war ended. The day I managed to get him to swing his legs over the side of the bed, one of his noisy neighbors proclaimed, "The war must be over, Joe has his feet out of bed." At this, the entire ward cheered and laughed at Joe's expense.*

*Five months have passed since I turned in my WAC uniforms, received my commission, and donned the uniform of a physical therapist. Before relating any more about my activities, I would like to pay tribute to the WACs— my nineteen months as an enlisted woman have been rich indeed and, when my patients discovered that I came up through the ranks, a common bond was established. It is easy to laugh now, when the difficult experiences along the way are but memories. Basic training in any branch of service teaches one to be tough both physically and mentally. I couldn't count the times over the past two years when I have said, "What a saving grace is a sense of humor."*

*Even before joining the WAC, physical therapy is something I often considered going into. But, at the time, felt that I couldn't afford to take a year off to get the training. Now, the Army has seen fit to give me the training. Pray that I may be worthy of their investment in me.*

The Day I Received My Commission

*To many of you, my life in the Army prob-ably sounds colorful and exciting. It is! But to try and convince you that I don't sometimes long for the quiet of yesteryear would be a lie. I have never met a person, regardless of their station or status in life who, at some time, has not gazed longingly at the grass on the other side of the fence. Right now, my dreams are to return to the wide open spaces of that farm I've talked so much about.*

*My hat is off to my fellow WAC's who work at monotonous, but necessary, jobs. It takes genuine strength of character to carry on in those positions and live the Army way. Give these girls the salute they deserve.*

*I am privileged to have and enjoy a pri-vate room. While living in a WAC's barracks I never suffered from lack of sleep; however, af-ter coming here, I slept the clock around for several nights. Our work is too tiring to permit frequent trips to New York during the week; therefore, imagine my embarrassment when I nearly fell* asleep *during an excellent play—**Life with Father.***

*Every day as we learn new technique, both doctors and patients are placing greater value on the benefits derived from physical therapy. I have found that I am doing just as much teaching now, as I work with my patients, as I did when I was teaching full time in the classroom. It is vital that our patients under-stand what it is we are hoping to accomplish with their treatment. Their cooperation, with confidence in their technician, is essential. Some patients returning to the hospital from fur-lough tell us how, by applying the knowledge they have learned in physical therapy, it helped them correct a physical condition in another family member.*

*Riding the Staten Island Ferry by day or night thrills me. I must admit that a number of times, rather than ask directions, I have boarded the wrong bus or subway and found myself far from my intended destination. I have learned a great deal about New York through trying to appear cosmopolitan.*

*On Sunday, having returned recently from a tour of the South Pacific, Daniel A. Poling, former Pastor of Marble Collegiate Church here in New York, spoke on the subject, "With McArthur and His Men." His address was an inspiration. When he said, "Friendship is one of the most profound experiences one can enjoy," it really caught my attention for it is impossible to put a dollar and cents value on friends. I consider my friends to be one of my biggest assets. Now, in addition to you who were my friends before I joined the WAC, I have added many more.*

*It will soon be two months since I returned from basic training with a large class of nurses at Atlantic City, but it wasn't anything as strenuous as our WAC basic training. All the lectures, training films, close order drills, and marches were repeat performances for me. My hands and arms got a good rest. In addition to the nurses attending, there were a group of hospital dieticians, and eight physical therapists. I composed the music to the following Physical Therapy song. The words, which express our sincere feelings toward physical therapy, were written by some of my classmates.*

### **Song of the Physical Therapy Corps**

*Beside our men on land and sea,*
*The P.T. Corps will stand.*

*To ease the sac-ri-fices made,*
*Re-build the lives they planned.*
*In this a life of strife and pain,*
*To have one job in view.*
*So al-to-ge-ther for one goal.*
*Come on, there's work to do!*

## *CHORUS*

*Hand in hand we'll always stand,*
*The P. T.'s in this war.*
*To treat the men who win the fight,*
*To strengthen and re-store.*
*Courage is the word they know!*
*We will do our part,*
*Over here and over there,*
*The Army P.T. Corps.*

*It was good to get home for Thanksgiving*
*and see so many friends and relatives again.*
*During the past year my course has been pretty*
*well charted but, from here on, anything can*
*happen. At least six of the girls who were in*
*school with me in Wisconsin last winter are now*
*stationed overseas. Frankly, I don't have any*
*definite ideas concerning that prospect for me;*
*however, my affairs and clothes are in such order*
*that I could move on very short notice.*

*Only last week I received a letter from*
*Frances. She is somewhere in France working*
*in a hospital tent. Although the tent is set up in*
*the middle of a cow pasture, she says it is clean*
*and well organized. I still enjoy every letter*
*that comes my way and hope that I'll be hear-*
*ing from you soon.*

*In celebrating this holiday season, I hope*

118

*to include some good theater entertainment. My best wishes to you for a Merry Christmas and a Happy New Year!*

*Yours for Victory,*
*Hazel V. Andrews*

## Letter 13

*September 29, 1945*
*Halloran General Hospital*
*Staten Island, New York*

*Dear Friends:*

*Many things have happened since I last wrote. We have had a very busy nine months. In many ways it seems that our work has been even more strenuous than that of the girls overseas. In the European theater, at least, the changes of the past several months have resulted in many of our field hospital units being placed on "stand by." Most of the patients have been evacuated to the States. Several girls, while awaiting orders, have written to tell me how they are "sweating out" an answer to their leave requests. Some of the girls have already returned home and are enjoying thirty days leave before having to report to their new duty assignments. As a result, the workload in the stateside hospitals has increased by such leaps and bounds that, for months, most of us have had very little time off.*

*One bright spot on the horizon is the possibility that some of the returning physical therapists will be assigned to supplement our staff. Confidentially, I have a selfish and ulterior motive in hoping this will happen—I am being*

119

*married soon and hope to be discharged from
the Army.*

*My fiance is Mr. Colman Quinn, a fine
Irishman who has been in the States now for
about twenty years. Colman, or "Jack" as I
call him, grew up in County Galway and received his degree in agriculture from the Royal
College of Science in Dublin. For a number of
years he applied his training in Upstate New
York; however, following an accident on the
farm and a long siege in the hospital, it became
necessary that he remain near the hospital for
further treatment. So, giving up his career in
agriculture, he secured a position as an auto-
mobile reconditioner—mine is human recondi-
tioning.*

*We both consider the country as the ideal
place to live but, for now, we will have to con-
tent ourselves with living in the heart of the
greatest metropolis in the world!*

*We are planning on a quiet wedding at my
home on the afternoon of October 13th. I hope
that many of you can come and also stay for
the reception that evening. I want you to meet
Jack and, of course, say hello to me.*

*Something tells me this will be my last let-
ter to you dealing with my Army career. After
writing this letter, I took the time to re-read my
other letters to you. It's surprising how much
has happened, how much water has gone over
the dam, since December of 1942 and the first
anniversary of Pearl Harbor.*

*I am sure that many G.I.'s share with me
the feeling that, though the years in service have
involved much sacrifice, we have all profited
by way of education and experience. I'm quite
sure, too, that we are all more tolerant and
broad-minded.*

*The American G.I. is tops and has a sense of humor that can't be surpassed. Like every man and woman in the service, I, too, am anxiously looking forward to returning to civilian life and being free of military discipline. I am also looking forward to marriage, establishing a home, and having Jack Quinn as my life partner, it makes an early discharge doubly inviting. Our address will be: 11 1/2 West 65th street, New York City, N.Y.*

*P.S.—Some of the other physical therapists have told me that, in view of my happy frame of mind, this letter sounds somewhat stilted. I have to admit that I have reveled in shopping for civilian clothes—especially my wedding dress. I am going to wear an afternoon dress, in fuchsia, with black accessories. It has been so much fun showing all of the pretty things to the girls. Many of them are married, but some are quite envious. I laugh and tell the younger girls that they were born thirty years too late.*

*Yours for a Happy Peace*

Hazel V. Andrews

# A Final Note Regarding My Military Service

*My months in the Army, particularly the long busy months at Halloran after I was commissioned, were gradually taking their toll. We provided care and treatment for every type of*

121

*injury imaginable. All casualties from the European theater passed through our hospital. Many of the men spent just a few days at Halloran before being transferred to a hospital that specialized in treating their particular problem or injury, whether it be burn, orthopedic, nerves, skin grafts, eye, or other.*

*A system was set up whereby a soldier's discharge was based on a point system with points awarded based on age, length of time in service, and other factors. Age alone would allow me an early discharge—I was 42 the fall of 1945.*

*I wanted out of the Army to get* married; *but, when I asked the head of our department, a much younger and very capable thereapist, she refused to process my discharge saying that I was needed there. In the meantime, however, I had been making definite plans to be married soon after my planned discharge date of October 1, 1945.*

### Discharge Papers

*Good fortune came my way when, out of a clear blue sky, she received orders to report for a week of detached service in Atlantic City leaving me in charge of the department. While she was away I applied for and was granted my discharge. When she returned from Atlantic City and found out what I had done, as one could expect, we had little to say to one another during my final days.*

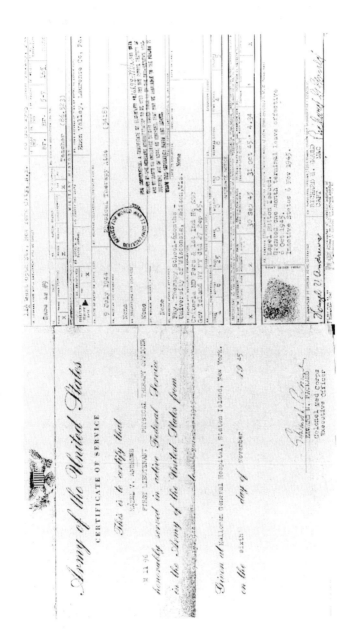

Discharge Papers

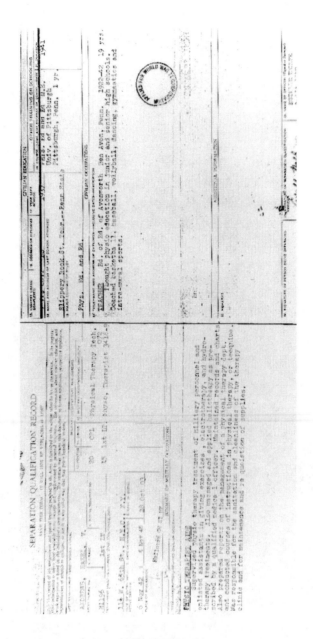

Discharge Papers

# PART III

## The Post World War II Years

As planned, Jack Quinn and I were married in my parents' home in Enon Valley, Pennsylvania on October 13, 1945.

We moved to New York City; but, just after World War II, good housing was at a premium; and we had to settle for a two-room and bath furnished apartment on the third floor of a walk-up brownstone in Manhattan. We had an ice box in the kitchen, and ice was delivered twice weekly. Within a month, I had secured a job as a physical therapist in Knickerbocker Hospital where the National Association for Infantile Paralysis maintained one entire floor. Polio vaccine was not yet in existence and we had many patients to care for. After several months in this depressing environment, I felt a need to be free from sick people for a while.

In September of 1946 I returned to teaching, traveling via subway and bus to Westwood, N.J. Then, in midsummer 1947, I received a telegram from a doctor who owned a small hospital in southern West Virginia offering me a good job in physical therapy. Jack was surprisingly agreeable—whatever I wanted, it seemed, he also wanted. Months later, I found out that he thought we were moving to Charlestown, West

Virginia where there is a horse-racing track. Ah me! In New York we had gone to horse races at both the Aqueduct and Belmont tracks; however, I didn't realize just how committed he was to the sport!

The hospital turned out to be a converted buff-brick school building. Shortly after arriving, the doctor asked us to move into the hospital where I would assume a leadership position. Thus, we moved from a room and board home into the goldfish bowl environment of the hospital.

Jack and I both worked very hard, he in an auto body and paint shop in Charleston, and I, at the hospital in nearby Marmet. We had no car, and this was before TV.

During this time we bought and refurbished an old eight room house in Enon Valley, converting it into two separate rental apartments. My Dad, more or less, supervised the refurbishing process including the cement work, wiring, carpentry, plumbing, installation of two bathrooms, the coal furnace, and the painting and papering.

Each apartment had four large rooms and a bath and, with everything being new, we had no problem finding tenants. We charged forty dollars per month for each apartment. When I told Dad what we were asking, he commented, "You'll scratch gravel a long time around Enon before you get that much rent." But all went well.

For the next year and a half we lived in West Virginia and then moved to Sewickley, Pennsylvania where I had secured a position in a nearby children's home and hospital. Jack, too, found work in Pittsburgh. However, we weren't happy with our jobs or our way of life—Jack had grown up on a farm in Ireland, and was educated as a farm agent—I, in Enon Valley. So we bought a hundred acre farm a few miles from Enon. We planned on raising chickens. I secured a teaching position in nearby Petersburg, Ohio. Neither Jack or I realized that farming in Enon would be so different from his farming experiences in Ireland. Poor Jack! He finally learned to operate a tractor, but he never did learn how to drive a car. In America, children have access to toys that teach them how to use tools and develop mechanical aptitude but, Jack, growing up in Ireland, lacked that advantage. I have said many times that, if he could fix anything by hitting it with a hammer, it was fixed! Ah, me!

We bought the farm from Amish people so our home had no modern conveniences. Our first order of business was to get it wired for electricity but, until then, we had to cook on an oil stove. For heat we used two coal heating stoves—one in the kitchen and the other in the living room. For light, we used oil lamps. What comfort! We used an outside privy for several months while waiting for our bathroom to be installed.

We started by buying day-old chicks in lots of 400 and soon learned the hard way that neither our chicken house nor our barn was warm enough to raise baby chicks. However, that condition was soon remedied when, one cold and snowy January night, the man who sold us our chicks told us that he had been offered a good job and was moving south. He insisted that we take receipt of the chicks a few days earlier than planned. After much soul-searching, we agreed to accept the 400 wee ones! We lived only on the first floor so, with the help of old newspapers, board partitions and heat from the first floor, we placed the baby chicks on the second floor where they thrived. Unfortunately, however, feathers began to replace their fuzzy yellow body covering. *Guess what happened to the fluffy yellow stuff?* It gravitated to the first floor, dispersing itself on our curtains, pictures, furniture, or wherever! Ah, me!

Later we learned to use electric brooders for the chicks' early stages of growth and, instead of the second floor, we kept them in the summer kitchen that adjoined the regular kitchen. Most of the time we kept the door separating the two kitchens open to provide extra dry heat for our little darlings.

One special pet, our cat, had the privilege of spending cold winter evenings in the warmth of our house. One night, while I was doing school work, she curled up at my feet under the kitchen table. At bedtime, when Jack picked up the broom to swish her toward the door, she refused to move. A closer inspection revealed why—she had delivered four kittens. Needless to say neither she nor her babies had to go outdoors. They rested comfortably in a lined box near the warmth of the kitchen stove.

Saturday was the day we usually made our weekly trip into East Palestine, Ohio to buy groceries and whatever else we needed for our chicks. One Saturday, Jack fixed the two coal stoves before we left home. We returned home just in time! Smoke was escaping around the kitchen door and windows. Quickly, Jack ran to the cellar for buckets of water. There was no fire; however, the wainscoting behind the kitchen stove was blistered and smoking. The house was full of smoke, and black soot had replaced the chicken fluff on all our belongings. The little chicks in the summer kitchen were in misery—many of them had suffocated. Jack removed the dead ones, and we hurried to get the place aired out. That evening I dissolved aspirin, added it to the chicks' drinking water and, picking them up, greased their little throats with Vicks' salve. How much good my medicine did we'll never know, but I felt better, and not many more chicks died.

Shortly, after cleaning up our home from the near fire, we resumed our normal life style. That is, if one could call it normal. Then along came a blizzard and we were snowbound for four days. That was the winter the western end of the Pennsylvania Turnpike was being completed. Thankfully, we had enough provisions for ourselves and the chickens, but we were snow bound.

All my life I had longed to live on a farm. Now, at the end of two years of teaching at Petersburg, Ohio, I resigned, determined to make it on the farm without my teacher's salary—or else! But by mid-October a friend of mine from New Castle, Pennsylvania came to call and told me that they were looking for another certified teacher in her building. I realized we needed the extra cash, so away I went.

After four years of teaching in New Castle, we sold our farm and Jack, taking a good position, moved back to New York. A teacher friend of mine from New Jersey advised me, "Get a teaching job in Long Island. That's where the good jobs are." She explained that, because the Leavit housing developments were in full swing in Nassau and Suffolk Counties, teachers were in great demand.

I had never been to Long Island and knew very little about it. During our four-day Easter vacation I drove to New York. Early that Good Friday morning, after Jack left for work, I drove my car to Great Neck in search of the administrator of Elementary Education. As I recall, the first name of the person who interviewed me was Hazel. It was an enjoyable and constructive interview. I learned that Great Neck didn't hire teachers who had less than four, nor more than ten, years of experience. At the conclusion of the interview, Hazel phoned a principal in Jericho, a town further out on the island, to make an appointment for me. A new school was opening that fall and they didn't have even one experienced teacher for the school. He offered me a job; however, I had the temerity to say, "I'm just shopping, could you suggest another school district where I might apply."

"I could send you to Hicksville, but I'm afraid they might offer you more money than we can."

"Where's Hicksville?" I asked.

After giving me directions, I assured him that I would let him know about his job offer.

It didn't take me long to find Hicksville and the school office. I was interviewed and hired at a salary considerably higher than that which I had been receiving in New castle.

Needless to say, I phoned and notified the principal in Jericho who had been so nice to me. Jack and I moved to Hicksville, where I remained from 1955 until 1971.

The room in which I was assigned to teach my third grade class was overcrowded because we had to share the room with a fifth grade class. The fifth grade reported at 7:30 a.m. and my students at 9:30 a.m. Fortunately, the different classes moved from room to room and we never had to share the home room at the same time. That fall, through the teachers union, I learned that our salaries were based on our education and years of experience and that the salary I was being paid was less than that prescribed by the union contract. An appointment with the Superintendent of Schools quickly brought about an adjustment in my salary; however, everything wasn't rosy. I had been teaching for twenty-six years and, up until that time, had never experienced any problems with an administrator. As all parties other than myself are long dead, I can safely say that I never taught for such a dogmatic, autocratic, dictatorial principal as that man.

After making an appointment with the Assistant Superintendent who had hired me, I poured out my unhappiness about the situation. Fearing that I was about to resign, he offered me a different position which I quickly accepted. Right after the Christmas holiday I moved into my new building. It was a good move—I felt at home. But, by 1963, I was fed up and exhausted.

In every lifetime, a time comes when one must cut the umbilical cord and reach out! There's a whole world out there and one can travel and take advantage of only a small portion of it. The message is, "Do it." Things don't always work out as planned but it is better to have tried and failed than it is to have never tried at all.

By the spring of 1963, as I have said, I thought I was burned out! We now had income coming in from several sources, so I quit teaching and Jack, at age 65, retired. We sponsored a cocktail party before a retirement dinner in a local restaurant. The day of the party I came home from school at noon and found Jack in bed sound asleep. He had started partying way too early—all forenoon! In desperation, I phoned our doctor who advised me to wake him up, give him some Dramamine, and lots of black coffee. Well it kicked in and, by the time we got to the restaurant, he was the life of the party. At dinner, when he was introduced, he stood up and sang, not one, not two, but three verses of *The Wearing Of The Green* and topped that off by inviting all in attendance to come home with us for what, in Ireland, is called a "Scraps Party." A good time was had by all. Ah, me!

During the winter of 1963-1964 Jack developed lung cancer. I have always said the Lord had a hand in having me quit my teaching position shortly before he was diagnosed for it would have been impossible for me to continue working and care for him, too. Unfortunately, surgery didn't help and he died in late May of 1965. In New York State, to qualify for retirement, a teacher must be teaching on his or her sixty-fifth birthday. So, after Jack's death, I returned and taught the necessary three years to qualify.

Having enjoyed good health for so many years, I have not been a complainer. I have seen people, including those I treated while in the Army who, even though they were born with handicaps, were still able to lead productive lives.

Most folks who live in the city can't comprehend why anyone would ever want to leave for life in the country. I would always give them something to think about when I would say, "Well, the only traffic problem one might encounter in Enon is an occasional herd of cattle crossing the road."

In October of 1971, on the week of my birthday, I decided to move back to Enon. Shortly after I returned home, I bought reservations for an extended excursion on a Norwegian freighter to the far east. Martha Anderson, Martha Hanna and my sister Ruth were going with me to make up a travel-

131

ing foursome for the November trip. However, a longshoremen's strike in New York changed our plans. When the day arrived for our departure, Arthur, my brother, drove the two Marthas and me to the Pittsburgh Airport where we boarded a plane for Montreal. From there we took a taxi to the harbor and boarded the freighter. We also met up with Ruth who had flown to Montreal from New York.

The day before Thanksgiving we sailed out of Montreal for our trip up the St. Lawrence River, down the East Coast, and through the Panama Canal. Ruth, unfortunately, fell off a deck chair and broke her collar bone. She could have gone ashore for treatment while we waited for our turn to go through the Canal, but was afraid the ship might leave without her. As if Ruth's misfortune was not enough, shortly before arriving in San Francisco, Martha Hanna slipped on the deck and broke her wrist. As soon as we docked, the shipping company took us to a medical clinic where my friends finally received treatment for their injuries.

That Christmas, the shipping company feted us by taking us first to Manila in the Philippines and then to Bangkok, Thailand where Ruth's son, Tom, lived. Before proceeding with the rest of our trip, Tom removed the heavy cast from Martha's wrist. While in Bangkok we visited a large beauty shop where, for a very nominal fee, I received a pedicure, manicure, a shampoo and a set from three beauty operators all working on me at the same time.

After visiting Chiang Mai, we traveled by train the entire length of the Malay Peninsula to Singapore. Throughout the long ride, we observed thousands of acres of flowers in full bloom—mostly brightly colored poppies. We carried our own food and drinking water on the train with us and many passengers slept on the floor in the aisles.

In Singapore, we were delighted to see our freighter; however, our delight was short lived when we went on board and were told that they already had twelve passengers—a full

Picture of Hazel with some of her purchases, following the five month freighter trip to the far east.

133

complement. If they had more than twelve, the law required that a doctor be on board—and they had no doctor. Imagine the feeling of being halfway around the world on a bright Sunday afternoon and not having a way home.

The shipping company paid for us to stay at the Hyatt Singapore. Then the next day, at our own expense, we moved into the YWCA—quite a contrast from the Hyatt. Thankfully, we were only there for three days. On Thursday they flew us to Penang, a South Pacific island where we boarded the original freighter that we had started our trip on. On April 22—Good Friday, after twenty days at sea, we arrived back in New York. We had been gone almost five months.

After renting a station wagon from Hertz we loaded our belongings and, before returning home to Pennsylvania, took Ruth to her home in Nyack, New York.

Because freighter companies refuse to take passengers aboard who are over eighty, this was the last of three such trips—trips that I so thoroughly enjoyed.

Somehow—somewhere—the notes of this trip and my other travels, along with the records of the cars I have owned, and papers about my teaching positions, have all disappeared; therefore, what is written here comes strictly from my memory. It saddens me to say that my three traveling companions on that long trip are no longer around to disagree with what I have written.

After leaving Ruth off at her home in New York state, we arrived in Enon. My home was newly refurbished and I had heat, electricity and water, but I still faced major decisions in the selection of carpeting, curtains, and other areas. Eventually, however, the place shaped up and I loved it.

Church activities and several local organizations took up much of my time. One of my favorite memories is that, for at least 50 years, the ladies of my home church, Enon Valley Presbyterian, have made apple butter in mid-October. The apples are donated by the Arnold family who have quite a sizable orchard. They make about 130 gallons in copper-lined kettles at the church parking lot. This project requires many hands. The apples must be washed, quartered, and cooked on the stove after which they are put through a large sieve. They are now ready for wooden stirrers. Some customers bring their own jars and lids. Some years ago, fruit jar lids were hard to come by. I wrote to the company that makes the lids. We received a big box of lids! That effort solved the problem. This annual project continues to this day.

Within a year of returning to Enon, I was busy laying the ground work for Chapter 1716 of the AARP which officially came into being in the late summer of 1973. The charter members included many retirees from Enon Valley and the nearby villages of New Galilee, and Darlington, as well as other nearby townships. The office of president fell onto my shoulders. We thrived! In fact, 1993 marked its 20th year; and they are still functioning as an effective group.

A year or so after returning to Enon, a large frame house across the street was being torn down. The owners intended to burn it after the demolition was completed; however, after I saw that one end of the house was an old log cabin that had been weather-boarded over, I bought it. I certainly didn't need a log house . . . but that is another story.

After buying the house, my neighbors agreed to carefully mark the logs north, east, south or west and number them from bottom to top to simplify putting it back together. For over a year, until I finally located someone to reconstruct the cabin, stacks of old logs stood on the lot. I first approached some Amish tradesmen to do the work; but they said the logs were too heavy. Finally, I located and hired a man who owned a backhoe to do the work.

Although, at the time, I was immersed in community activities, with the help of many people, my log cabin materialized. We installed a cement slab under the flooring and located some excellent cut stone for the entrance. At first, I

Hazel Staining Flooring for Cabin

thought I would have to buy new flooring; however, upon close inspection of the existing aged flooring, I found it to be usable. Unfortunately, it had, over the years, been painted either terra-cote or blue; but, with a mixture of salt, soda and ammonia, many days, and a whole lot of elbow grease, I was able to remove the old paint. Later, I added a thin layer of oil which brought out and highlighted the original grain of the wood. It was now a genuine patina and looked as though it belonged. The rafters for my cabin came from an old log house near St. Clairsville, Ohio, where land was being cleared away for coal stripping. The pairs of hand-hewn rafters had numbers written in Roman numeral style at one end and holes for wooden pegs on the same end as the numbers. Many of the details of reconstruction required time and patience.

During the time the cabin and furnishings were evolving, I made several trips to the New Castle Public Library to read books about the lives of the people who came to this wild unsettled country. I found that the first free school law was passed in 1834 and that the Hartshorn School in Darlington Township was in operation 1807-1908. It was named for Mr. Hartshorn, a bachelor, and the founder and first teacher at the school. Also, among the first teachers were Sampson Dilworth and Joshua Newell. They had few, if any, school supplies and parents paid for their children's education by providing room and board for the teacher for several weeks during the school year.

Many visitors, including clubs and organizations from Beaver Valley and New Castle, came to see the cabin after its completion. For these visits I recorded the story of the cabin and supplemented the taped message with personal comments.

Old broom handles served as curtain rods for the unbleached muslin curtains; a cradle, containing a doll dressed in a 100 year old christening dress, and a desk from a nearby country school were a part of the furnishings for the cabin. The following is a partial listing of the other furnishings that were provided by many people and from many sources:

| | |
|---|---|
| 1. A trestle table | 13. Hinges & Latches |
| 2. Benches | 14. Braided rugs |
| 3. Corner Cupboard | 15. Wooden spoons |
| 4. Churn | 16. Iron kettle |
| 5. Wooden bowls | 17. Crockery bean pot |
| 6. Lindsey Woolsey Wall Hanging | 18. Teacher's desk |
| 7. Ceiling angle lamp | 19. Rocking chair caned seat |
| 8. Dry sink | 20. Wheel for spinning wheel |
| 9. An old mirror | 21. High chair (by grandfather McCown) |
| 10. Shaving brush & cup | 22. Flat Iron |
| 11. Razor strap | 23. Candle Mold |
| 12. Wrought iron door | 24. Miscellaneous items |

Below two of the windows were wooden window boxes that, in season, held petunias and geraniums. There was a sheepskin hanging on the wall. I enjoyed telling the visitors, at least those who looked like they might believe it, that it was the skin of a wolf that was killed in an area between Enon and Darlington known as "Hells' Hollow."

The Cabin

While living in my little house in Enon (beside the log cabin), I instituted a plan to pay for needed improvements on the Church. It was my wish to keep these gifts anonymous. With the full cooperation of the Pastor, Rev. Ray Gausman, I eventually contributed $5,000 to the Improvement fund. All organizations within the Church cooperated. Rev. Gausman was informed and, as each thousand was raised; he would inform me, and I would pass on to him a thousand dollars. This really brought the different organizations within the Church together.

During these months, my brother told me folks thought I was the contributor. My response to him, "People have said as much to me . . . whatever gave them that idea?"

I don't consider myself a wealthy woman and have worked hard all my life. In the eyes of some people, I need newer clothes and furniture. Growing up, I learned to watch every nickel. That training and practice in early life continues. Monthly, I send money to the Enon Church. I support Habitat for Humanity and other worthy causes.

As I, once again, read the following letter from the Enon Valley United Presbyterian Church, dated January 24, 1977, written in response to my contribution, I know it was part of God's plan for my life:

*Dear Benefactor,*

*The congregation of the Enon Valley United Presbyterian Church would like to take this opportunity to express its gratitude for the lavish generosity you have shown us in the past year. The healthy Special Improvement Fund we now have to work with will mean that much needed remodeling can be done. Big changes will soon be made in the church social room and other projects will also be undertaken.*

*Your unexpected offer early last year has re-*

*sulted in more than just a sizable amount of money to work with, as important and pleasant as that is. Your challenge caused us to unite and work together in a very special way to reach our goal. The hard work, spirit of cooperation, and fellowship experienced in the past months have led to a real sense of accomplishment as a church and as individuals.*

*It seems very strange to be saying, "Thank you" for so much to someone we know only as our "benefactor." Our gratitude and appreciation are no less heart-felt because of that, however. The Enon Church is "richer" in a number of important ways because you have shown such an interest in us. We will always be grateful.*

*Sincerely,*

Our monthly AARP meetings were held in the Enon Valley Fire Hall. Social enjoyment of the brown bag lunch that always preceded the program was well received by all who attended. At one of the meetings I happened to mention that I was looking for some ferns to plant near the cabin. Jim Reed, the man sitting across the table from me, heard me and said he had just what I was looking for. A few days later, true to his word, he not only brought the ferns to my home, he even planted them for me. That was the start of a close relationship. Even though both of us were wary of making a permanent commitment, we did, and were married on August 26, 1978 in my little house near the cabin. Jim laughingly told his friends that his father had died at age seventy-nine; and here he, at the age of 80 was getting married to a young woman of seventy-five.

In 1980, I sold my little house and, in 1982, Jim sold his trailer and one hundred wooded acres. My husband had a strange affinity with nature—one that was admirable. For example, a bee could crawl all over his face, hands, and arms but wouldn't sting him. In the summer of 1981, while we were at his cabin, we observed a family of raccoons that lived in the nearby woods. Every evening they would come to our porch to beg for the shelled corn that Jim fed them.

Jim always maintained a good rapport with the men who worked for him at Bell Telephone of Pennsylvania. He always had a story to fit any occasion. One former employee, after Jim's death, shared with me the first story he had ever heard Jim tell. Jim said, "Up around Clarion, where I grew up, the people are so healthy they had to shoot a man just to start a cemetery."

In the fall of 1988, Jim and I moved into Woodland Retirement Village in Bradenton. Although Jim had never been to Florida, we enjoyed each other's company for ten wonderful years in our double-wide home. We especially enjoyed swimming and sitting together at the swimming pool. Soon after this he became ill and was in a nursing home for fifteen months prior to his death in December 1990. Even though I continue to live in Bradenton, I claim Enon as my home—it is where my roots are firmly planted.

A lot has happened since 1904 when I moved with my family to Enon. All over America there are small towns, burgs, and villages similar to Enon. Unfortunately, many of these no longer have the tax base that is needed to keep up with their needs. Such was the case in 1993 in Enon. All the sidewalks were cracked, broken, and in bad need of repair or replacement. In June of 1993, I wrote to the city council and expressed a desire to pay for having the sidewalks repaired. Then I wrote another letter to Ed Powers of the Enon Valley Council on June 28, 1993, saying:

> *If I live through October 28, 1993, I'll be 90 years old. Because of my age, action on this proposal should not be delayed. When my ashes are*

*laid to rest in Little Beaver Cemetery, I will be the*
*last of four generations of Andrews who have*
*called Enon Valley "home."*

Although the project was slow in getting started, it was completed in December of 1995, and put a new face on Main street. It pleased me to be able to return something to the village that, for so many years, had meant so much to me.

When I moved back to Enon Valley from Long Island, New York, in 1971, many friends and some relatives of my vintage were still living in the area. It is now many years later and most of my friends and family members have died. The fall that I was 90, I arranged for the ladies of my Church in Enon Valley to serve a luncheon to my cousins, etc. My invitations to them stated the time, place, and purpose. There were to be no gifts. I stated that my needs were limited largely to prescriptions and liniments! There were 40 in attendance. The previous Sunday the preacher announced that there would be open house in the Church social rooms that afternoon. About 40 more came; such a joyful day! One car brought former pupils from Emsworth. Cousins Ralph and Mary Veon transported me to and from the airport, housed me, and entertained me royally throughout my stay.

A message on one of my birthday cards expresses a truth. "There is only trouble with getting older; "By the time we reach greener pastures, we can't find the darn fence."

In May of 1995, I had the misfortune to fall in my apartment. Many days in the hospital and weeks in the Rehabilitation Center were very helpful. A mechanized cart has replaced the wheelchair and other equipment I originally had to use. But I'm not complaining, because, as I have previously said, I have seen many people with physical handicaps who have gone on to lead productive lives. Like the old man who visited his Doctor and said, "I eat good, I sleep good, but I have no desire to work." That's me!

Since my fall, my journeys from Woodland Retirement Home are limited; however, I have told many people that I am glad it is the foot-end of me that is less than 100 percent rather than the head-end. (I think). Because I do very little buying, I am investing in computers for the elementary schools in the Blackhawk School District near Beaver Falls, PA. This school district serves my hometown, the Enon Valley area. I know nothing about computers, but the present and coming generations had better get on board. When I attended Enon Valley High School almost 75 years ago, our science department consisted of little more than a galvanized bucket, a soup plate, and a Bunsen burner. Although I am probably over-stating the case, it makes a good story.

What I have written barely scratches the surface of my total experiences; but I believe that it at least provides you, the reader, with some insight into *My Twentieth Century*. At my present age, just reviewing these chapters of my life makes me weary but, after reviewing what I have written, I would have to say that my philosophy of life can be summarized in just two words—"keep moving."

Picture Taken on my 93rd birthday— October 28, 1996

Picture of Hazel with First Husband—Jack Quinn

Picture of Hazel with Second Husband—Jim Reed